BWB Texts

Short books on big subjects
for Aotearoa New Zealand

Abolishing the Military
Arguments and Alternatives

GRIFFIN MANAWAROA LEONARD,
JOSEPH LLEWELLYN AND
RICHARD JACKSON

Contents

Introduction

There is no question that we live in a dangerous and insecure world. In early 2022, as we were writing this book, Russia invaded Ukraine, highlighting the ever-present threat of full-scale military invasion from hostile states. Recent great power rivalry such as that between the United States and China, weakening arms control agreements, nuclear proliferation, the trade in light weapons, persistent authoritarianism and the spread of different forms of violent extremism underline the seemingly perennial threat of political violence. At the same time, the pandemic, the climate crisis, extreme levels of inequality, mass migration and refugee movements, the rise of populism, cyber-crime and the spread of disinformation and conspiracy theories are adding to social instability and political volatility around the world. In Aotearoa New Zealand, wealth inequality, poverty, distributive injustice, crime, rising polarisation and the failure to reconcile the ongoing impacts of colonisation pose real and ongoing challenges to social stability, individual wellbeing and security.

For most people, the obvious response to this uncertain security environment and the myriad threats facing the nation includes the military and security approaches we have depended on in the past – a strong and professional military, alliances with great powers, involvement in peacekeeping operations, deploying military units to fight with overseas partners when needed and generally acting as a 'good international citizen'. Belief in the necessity and effectiveness of military force to keep our nation safe and secure is nothing less than common sense in Aotearoa New Zealand, as it is virtually everywhere in the world. But is this belief in the military justified, or is it an explanatory story we have internalised without it necessarily being true – a myth, in other words?

When we describe something as a 'myth', we are not implying that it is purely fictional or necessarily irrational; we might also call it a common-sense belief or collective narrative. We are instead pointing to its socially assumed and unquestioned nature, and to the role it plays in a society's collective beliefs and culture, particularly in terms of national identity. Myths are the stories we tell ourselves as a society that help to define who we are and justify the way we live, and they are embedded in numerous areas of society, including the political system. They can be a complex mix of facts, history, assumptions and beliefs. In many cases, they contribute to rigid ways of thinking about a problem and inhibit reflection and continued critical assessment.

This book takes critical aim at what we have chosen to call the 'myth of military security'. We seek to prompt broader public, political and academic debate about Aotearoa New Zealand's historically embedded approach to national defence and security. What does it mean to be secure in today's global threat environment, and are today's threats the same as those of bygone decades? What does genuine national security entail, anyway, and how should we measure or assess it? More importantly, what is the best means or method to achieve security and defend the nation, and what are the costs and benefits of relying on military force to do so? If military force is less useful in responding to emerging threats like climate change or pandemics, or insufficient to protect us from cyber-attacks and terrorism, what other non-military approaches to security should we consider?

We argue that an honest and scrupulous analysis of the evidence will show that the widely held idea that we need a military to ensure defence and security is questionable; it's more myth than reality, a comforting but misleading story from a bygone era. Moreover, the purported benefits of possessing a military are likely outweighed by the costs and dangers of maintaining and using such forces. We argue that it would be better to abolish the New Zealand Defence Force Te Ope Kātua o Aotearoa (NZDF), replace it with more effective and more appropriate institutions and processes, and consider alternative security paradigms that can meet current and future threats and dangers, and positively contribute to peace, democracy and wellbeing.

We are not the first to make this case, and we won't be the last. There have been numerous anti-militarist movements in Aotearoa's history, including by Māori groups who opposed forcible settler colonisation with campaigns of nonviolent resistance. Perhaps the first major anti-militarist movements in New Zealand's history emerged in opposition to New Zealand troops being sent to fight in the South African War in 1899 and then to the Defence Act of 1909, which mandated compulsory military training for almost all men and boys. These movements contributed in turn to the conscientious objector movements in the two world wars. Later, anti-militarism took the form of the anti-Vietnam War movement and the anti-nuclear movement, which had a major success in its limited goal of making New Zealand nuclear-free. Wider efforts over the decades seeking unilateral disarmament or the abolition of the military failed to gain traction – largely because, following World War I, the Anzac myth solidified as the central political and cultural narrative about the role of the military in the birth of New Zealand's national identity. It proved extremely difficult for later generations to shift.

Given the centrality of the Anzac myth and the military to the nation's foreign relations, history, culture and sense of identity, we understand that the abolition of the NZDF will seem like an extreme proposal to most people. But in a calcified system experiencing changing threats, sometimes extreme proposals are required. How we choose to pursue our security and defence has enormous ethical, political and financial consequences, and relying on old myths and assumptions to make our choices will not do. There should be rigorous public debate about foreign policy and international affairs, about whether we ought to maintain our military forces and alliances, and about whether there are genuine alternatives. We find it surprising, even somewhat alarming, how little public discussion there has been concerning the real costs and benefits, as well as the efficacy and ethics, of military defence and its alternatives. Here, we hope to change that.

We want to make it clear at the outset that our criticisms are not targeted at individual members of the NZDF. The NZDF is staffed by many fine people who, like all of us, hope that their work will support their whānau and make positive contributions to our communities. Rather, our criticisms are of the NZDF as an institution – its funding, composition and raison d'être – as well as the political processes that continue to prioritise military defence over other socially beneficial spending.

The aim of this book is to subject the largely unquestioned and unexamined acceptance of military force and military-based approaches to security and national defence in Aotearoa to critical examination. In Chapter 1, we look at the cost, composition, training, equipment and foreign policy and defence roles of Aotearoa's military forces, and the assumptions and beliefs that many people hold about the NZDF. We scrutinise whether the costs of the NZDF are justified in the current threat environment, whether some of its key roles and responsibilities, such as disaster relief or humanitarian assistance, could be undertaken by better-trained and -equipped actors, and whether it is well suited to contemporary threats and dangers or to Aotearoa's aspirations to conduct an independent and principled foreign policy.

In Chapter 2, we examine Aotearoa's security paradigm – the way it defines, conceptualises and responds to threats and dangers, and what it considers national security to entail. We explore the nature of contemporary threats, such as pandemics and the climate crisis, to determine whether military-based security approaches which rely on weaponry, soldiers, the use of force and alliances are really the best guarantee of national security in today's world, and whether there are alternative, more effective and more ethical approaches to national security.

In Chapter 3, we take an honest look at the outcomes of Aotearoa's many overseas military engagements, scrutinising whether they have made a real contribution to peace, stability and democracy in the world. We ask a critical question rarely posed: what does the evidence show about whether military force actually works to make a more peaceful world? In this case, what does the evidence show about Aotearoa's involvement in international peacekeeping, its contribution to US- or Anglosphere-led wars and its role in the continuing global war on terror? Have any of these deployments contributed to making Aotearoa safer and more secure, and have they contributed to making a safer, more secure international system?

In Chapter 4, we examine the alternatives to military force. If military force has proven to be ill-equipped to deal with current threats, is limited in the kinds of national security it can deliver and has a history of failure in creating peace and security, are there any alternatives – and what is the evidence such alternatives would work any better? In this chapter, we examine the growing evidence for unarmed civilian peacekeeping, civilian-based social defence, nonviolent resistance and other forms of non-traditional security. We explore whether alternative approaches to security, and alternative foreign policy postures, could provide wider and deeper kinds of security for the people of Aotearoa, and we briefly look at states that have chosen to abolish their military to see what happened afterwards.

In the conclusion, we weigh up the arguments and evidence for abolishing the NZDF and adopting a new security approach. We also consider the objections that will no doubt be raised to our arguments in this book. Some will insist, for example, that there are other important benefits to having a military apart from national defence, and that our obligations as a responsible international citizen require the possession and maintenance of a military. Others will simply assert that there are no serious alternatives to military force, the military is an essential part of our national identity and abolishing it is politically impossible in any case. Yet others will demand to know how exactly such a revolutionary transformation could be practically undertaken.

The purpose of this book is not to make a foolproof, irrefutable argument which can account for every objection or convince every sceptic. Nor is it to present a detailed blueprint for transitioning Aotearoa away from its reliance on the military. Rather, we simply hope to present a series of arguments and some evidence which demonstrate that our current national defence and security approach is seriously flawed, most likely contributes to insecurity rather than security, and is based on a series of unexamined beliefs or myths. More importantly, we also hope to demonstrate that realistic, credible alternatives to military-force-based national security exist and should be seriously considered by policymakers, academics and the public.

In other words, we hope to contribute to an important national conversation with some arguments and perspectives that are all-too-often missing from serious discussions on foreign policy. It is difficult to have a completely full and open public discussion about the military because there are limitations on publicly available information about its role and activities. But this is the very reason debate should be undertaken: what the military does on behalf of the nation must be up for democratic scrutiny. And as we demonstrate in the following pages, there is more than enough publicly available information for a rigorous debate.

1. The Myth of the New Zealand Defence Force

It is widely assumed that the New Zealand Defence Force is needed for national defence, security and meeting our obligations as a good international citizen, and that either the force is already trained and equipped to deal with the threats and dangers facing Aotearoa New Zealand today or that it should be given even more resources to support that mission. But what are the extent and nature of the current threats facing Aotearoa? More importantly, how do our political and military leaders assess the present threat environment? A fortunate consequence of several interrelated factors, including our geographical isolation and lack of hostile neighbours, is that Aotearoa New Zealand is unlikely to experience any major attempt to have its sovereignty overthrown or territory invaded in a similar way to the Russian invasion of Ukraine in 2022. The Ministry of Defence's *Defence Assessment 2014* reported that:

New Zealand does not presently face a direct threat of physical invasion and occupation of New Zealand territory. The likelihood of such a threat to the Cook Islands, Niue, Tokelau and territory over which we have a sovereign claim, emerging before 2040 is judged to be very low, and would be preceded by significant change to the international security environment. New Zealand could therefore expect to have a reasonable amount of time to re-orientate its defence priorities should this be necessary.[1]

Subsequent defence assessments have not signalled any significant change in this broad assessment. For example, the 2021 assessment, which notes that the international security environment is worsening, nevertheless states:

> [W]e consider New Zealand does not yet face a direct military threat to the territory of New Zealand itself, and judge that any such threat would almost certainly only emerge in the context of a major war. We do agree, however, with the judgement in Australia's *2020 Defence Strategic Update* that the prospect of major armed conflict in the Indo-Pacific is less remote than it has been.[2]

In other words, it is assessed that although the chances of war in the Indo-Pacific are 'less remote' than in the past, such a threat is not deemed to be a leading concern by the Ministry of Defence (MoD). The Australian strategic update referenced here states that while the chances of armed conflict in the region are less remote, it is still unlikely.[3] Moreover, the term 'Indo-Pacific' references a larger ecosystem of nations and regions that includes East Asia, the Pacific, the Indian subcontinent and the Pacific Rim, well beyond what many New Zealanders would think of as our immediate Pacific neighbourhood.[4] Thus, it is entirely possible that in the unlikely event of a military conflict, it could play out in the Indo-Pacific region but without taking place in the Pacific, let alone threatening New Zealand territory directly.

Instead, the *Defence Assessment 2021* identifies the two most pressing threats to Aotearoa's security as broader strategic competition within the Indo-Pacific and Pacific regions, and climate change.[5] Strategic competition, the assessment asserts, is seen in the increased number of states that are challenging the norms of the so-called rules-based order that has existed since the end of the Cold War. The 2021 assessment makes clear that this international order, ostensibly based on liberal economics and democracy (what is often called the post-war liberal order), has historically been underwritten by the United States. China and Russia are discussed as the primary challengers to this order, with China's increased involvement in the Pacific highlighted.[6] The United States, following the election of Joe Biden, is committed to bolstering its influence in the Pacific region.[7] With Chinese and US interests in the Pacific seen to be at odds, it is argued that many states are seeing a decreased ability to navigate a middle path between the two powers.

At the same time, climate change will produce its own risks and dangers, while also exacerbating the challenges presented by geo-strategic competition. Environmental degradation, rising sea levels and extreme weather events will likely lead to an increase in the number and intensity of humanitarian disasters. As the NZDF's *Climate Crisis: Defence Readiness and Responsibilities* report notes, the Pacific region is likely to be disproportionately impacted by such trends. Additionally, '[w]hen the effects of climate change intersect with a complex array of environmental and social issues, they can be significant contributors to both low-level and more violent conflict.'[8] Climate change, it is feared, could lead to violent competition for diminishing resources, whether these be food, water, land or fuels. Violence could also stem from mismanaged adaptation or migration in response to adverse climate change effects.

These challenges are large, amorphous and, in the case of climate change, cannot be attributed to a specific actor. A core argument of recent MoD and NZDF publications is that security challenges will increasingly play out in 'the grey zone'. This is understood as:

> [T]he space between peace and war that spans coop-eration, competition, confrontation and conflict . . . .
> Actors engaging in grey zone activities seek to create or exploit uncertainty, which can shape others' perceptions around risks of escalation, including thresholds for armed conflict. These activities provide states with a level of plausible deniability, are not well addressed in international law, and hinder others' abilities to react, including in space, cyber-space and the high seas.[9]

Many of the specific threats facing Aotearoa high-lighted in recent MoD and NZDF reports are described as 'complex disruptors', some of which are manifestations of the strategic competition mentioned above. These complex disruptors are 'transnational trends and devel-opments that challenge international stability in complex ways'.[10] They include the malevolent use of technological advancements in artificial intelligence or cyber capabilities, competition in space, violent extremism (which is noted to have decreased steadily since 2014), transnational crime and fragile states. It is noted that some grey zone activities are particularly difficult for democratic political systems to deal with because democratic governments do not, for example, have much control over the internet or other public domains, thereby lessening their ability to counter foreign interference or extremist ideologies. Thus, not only are some actors challenging the norms of liberal democracy by asserting alternative forms of governance, but their tactics are also designed to exploit and undermine democratic governance within democracies.

The relationship between grey zone activities and the likelihood of military conflict is difficult to determine. As both the New Zealand and Australian defence forces have noted, a defining feature of grey zone activities is that they attempt to advance a state's interest *without* engaging an adversary in armed combat. Yet, because grey zone activities represent broader strategic competition and some employ a 'military-civilian fusion' approach in which military forces or resources back apparently civilian undertakings, the risk of military conflict is potentially increased.[11] Australian and New Zealand assessments of security in the Pacific note the potential for combat being accidentally triggered. This combat would most likely play out at sea, the 2021 assessment states.[12] Specific hypothetical threats that are most alarming to the MoD include:

- the establishment of a military base or dual-use facility in the Pacific by a state that does not share New Zealand's values and security interests;
- extra-regional military-backed resource exploitation in the Pacific;
- military confrontation generally, as may play out between other parties in the Pacific for the above-noted reasons;
- and contested responses to security events, such as competition and contestation for regional influence during natural disaster or internal instability events affecting Pacific countries.[13]

Looming over all of this is the fear that increased humanitarian demands stemming from climate change might over-stretch NZDF resources. As *The Climate Crisis* report puts it:

> The impacts of climate change are being felt acutely in the Pacific as well as in New Zealand itself. This will necessitate more humanitarian assistance and disaster relief and stability operations in our region .... New Zealand may be faced with concurrent operational commitments, which could stretch resources and reduce readiness for other requirements.[14]

In sum, the central contention of the New Zealand government's assessment of Aotearoa's security is that while there is no direct military threat to the country's territory, growing competition between major powers and the increased propensity for this competition to play out in the grey zone threatens the international and regional stability that Aotearoa has long benefited from. These competitive effects also challenge international norms of human rights and governance that most New Zealanders value. Transnational terrorism and crime further challenge these norms, as the associated groups (and their ideologies), by definition, disregard national borders. Climate change exacerbates the situation, while also creating issues of resource scarcity and, potentially, mass migration.

These assessments of the regional and global security environment are useful, but because they are based on a narrow set of assumptions this usefulness is limited. They ignore, for example, the reasonable argument that the very degradation of international norms and stability that now constitutes one of the biggest perceived threats to Aotearoa's security is, in large part, a product of countries, including New Zealand, responding to the threat of terrorism and violent extremism through military means in the so-called global war on terror. It is no coincidence that, as the *Defence Assessment 2021* notes, the 'high-water mark' of democratic norms occurred in the early 2000s and has been declining ever since:

> After reaching a high-water mark in the early 2000s, overall global adherence to democratic norms has been declining. This ranges from increases in nationalist sentiment, through reversals in previous trends toward greater liberalism, to a narrowing of the civil society space. Globally, moves away from democracy within

individual states contribute to weakening the basis and support for the values and norms that underpin the international rules-based system.[15]

No one would deny that there are threats to Aotearoa's security. No country is, or can be, 100 per cent secure. The question is: with limited resources at our disposal, which threats are most detrimental to New Zealanders' security, and how might we as a nation best address them? Is the institution that is currently tasked with the defence of Aotearoa, the NZDF, the best designed and equipped to deal with those threats? Are there more efficient, cost-effective and ethical means of providing for the security of New Zealanders in the current complex threat environment?

A Defence Force, for Combat

The NZDF came into being under the Defence Act 1990, but its historical origins lie in the colonial period when a mixture of British imperial troops, local militia and later an armed constabulary provided the force necessary for suppressing internal threats to the emerging settler society. The Militia Ordinance of 1845, for example, allowed for the formation of local battalions, while the Armed Constabulary was formed in 1846. The Colonial Defence Force Act 1862 took another step towards military consolidation in the territory, but it wasn't until the Defence Act of 1909 that a unified territorial military force was created. Up to this point, the various forces were primarily used to attack and suppress

Māori, and they played a key role in the invasion and confiscation of Māori land. It was only around the turn of the nineteenth century that New Zealand troops began to play a role in foreign wars, primarily in support of the British Empire.

Today, the NZDF is made up of three branches: the New Zealand Army Ngāti Tūmatauenga; the Royal New Zealand Navy Te Taua Moana o Aotearoa; and the Royal New Zealand Air Force Te Tauaarangi o Aotearoa. As of 8 June 2023, there were 15,236 employees of the NZDF. Civilian workers account for 3,060 employees, while the regular and reserve forces account for 8,726 and 3,450, respectively. Navy, Army and Air Force total 2,813, 6,519 and 2,844 personnel, respectively.[16] Globally speaking, the NZDF is very small. China, North Korea and the United States have approximately 2.33 million, 1.19 million and 1.38 million military personnel, respectively.[17] Further, Aotearoa lacks the means of substantially increasing its military power, relative to other countries, due to its relatively small population and limited financial and mineral resources.

The NZDF has stated for years that its mission is 'to secure New Zealand against external threat, to protect our sovereign interests, including in the Exclusive Economic Zone, and to be able to take action to meet likely contingencies in our strategic area of interest'.[18] In pursuing this objective, the NZDF undertakes a variety of activities, including disaster relief efforts internationally and domestically, overseas combat operations, multinational peacekeeping operations and support for scientific enquiry in the Antarctic. While these activities are diverse, they are not all equally as important to the NZDF's existence or identity.

Primarily, the NZDF is a force for armed combat, and its financial and human resources are allocated with this purpose in mind. The NZDF has always been clear about its purpose, even if this aspect is often downplayed in the public sphere in favour of benevolent peacekeeping or disaster response roles about which the public feels very positive. As a former Chief of the NZDF, Lieutenant General T.J. Keating, said in the NZDF's *Statement of Intent 2015–2018*:

> Our purpose is to provide the government of-the-day
> with credible and effective options to deliver an armed
> response when New Zealand's interests are at stake.
> So first and foremost, we are a Force prepared for
> combat. This is our raison d'etre.[19]

Similarly, the *Strategic Defence Policy Statement* for 2018 states: 'The core task of the Defence Force is to conduct military operations, in particular combat operations. The Defence Force maintains a range of capabilities for the delivery of combat effects on both land and at sea'.[20] Or note the central mission of the Army, as quoted on its website and in *Army25: Chief of Army's Brief*: 'To provide world-class combat ready land forces that are trained, led and equipped to win as part of an Integrated Defence Force.'[21]

Moreover, as detailed later in the 2015–18 statement of intent, the forces are held principally to allow the NZDF to respond to security events in which New Zealand acts alone to protect national interests. By its own words, and contrary to what some in Aotearoa assume or prefer to forget, the NZDF exists primarily to carry out *unilateral* armed operations rather than multinational missions. This purpose is reiterated in many MoD and NZDF publications, including the 2018–21 and 2021–24 statements of intent.[22]

Defending New Zealand?

Many New Zealanders believe that the NZDF exists primarily to defend the territorial sovereignty of Aotearoa – the very name implies this purpose. (So too does its name in te reo Māori, Te Ope Kātua o Aotearoa, meaning 'the line of defence of New Zealand'.) Certainly, defence of a nation's citizenry from unprovoked attack by a foreign invader doesn't appear to raise the same moral conundrums as deciding which international conflicts to participate in. Yet, as we saw above, Aotearoa does not currently face a threat to its territorial sovereignty, and such a threat materialising in the foreseeable future is unlikely. Moreover, later in this chapter we show that much of the NZDF's work is carried out far from Aotearoa, in areas such as the Middle East.

A crucial question remains, however: how effective would the NZDF be in defending us from a foreign aggressor? The answer is not very. Because of Aotearoa's extreme geographic isolation, relatively large and varied landscape and good international standing, only an extremely committed and capable aggressor would attempt (or even be able to attempt) an invasion, in which case we would be facing a nation many times more militarily powerful than ourselves. As mentioned above, in comparison to other countries, Aotearoa's military is very small, as is our industrial base in sectors required to continue military resistance, such as petroleum production. As noted, New Zealand has geographic features that would make it difficult to invade, but these features also present challenges to a military defence of our territory. For example, our isolation by way of being a remote island also means we have 15,000 kilometres of coastline that would require defending. Repelling an invasion before an aggressor could get a foothold would be practically impossible.

Once an invading power had established a military base or bases in Aotearoa, it would attempt to implement an occupation. Military victory is not the end goal of an invading force. Rather, an invader typically wants to, for example, extract resources, seize land and/ or exercise political control. These would require more than just the military defeat of Aotearoa. To achieve this, an occupying force would, among other things, need to seize or build infrastructure and put in place puppet politicians and political processes to substantiate a claim to sovereignty. Ultimately, this would require the subjugation of Aotearoa's population, as their labour would still be needed in vital industries and their participation in the political system required to project a legitimate claim to sovereignty over the territory. Alternatively, an invader could encourage or force large-scale immigration from its own territory to New Zealand to serve these purposes.

In either case, the NZDF is not equipped to meet these realities of invasion. Following the initial phase of attempting to repel an invader, it would be depleted. Lives would have been lost and our already low troop numbers would be devastated. The adversary's greater and more advanced military technology, such as its weapon systems and vehicles, would have depleted our own, adding to the discrepancy in this regard. In such a condition, the NZDF would not be able to effectively carry out the tasks required to resist or overthrow an occupation which would involve, among many other things, safeguarding or defending citizens from harm, sabotaging vital industry and creating alternative community and political arrangements by which New Zealanders could communicate and organise to resist the occupation. In Chapter 4, we explain how civilian-based defence is arguably better suited to these realities of invasion and occupation.

In fact, the New Zealand government and some members of the public recognise that the NZDF could not defend Aotearoa from full-scale invasion or occupation. Regarding the territorial defence of Aotearoa New Zealand, the *Defence Assessment 2021* acknowledges that:

> New Zealand would very likely require substantial assistance from partner nations to deter or defeat any such military threat [against our sovereign territory] (the last such threat was during World War Two). The independent territorial defence of New Zealand should not therefore be the principal driver for New Zealand's defence policy.[23]

As a consequence, the NZDF and Aotearoa's defence policy have not been designed with this goal in mind. In the foreign policy section of this chapter, and in other parts of this book, we will discuss what the NZDF is actually used for, and assess the likelihood that 'partner nations' would come to our aid in the event of military threat.

Funding the New Zealand Defence Force

Historically, the NZDF has been comparatively well funded and well resourced in carrying out its functions. In 2021, according to the Stockholm International Peace Research Institute and the World Bank (different sources quote slightly different numbers), Aotearoa New Zealand's military spending was $4.79 billion.[24] After adjusting for inflation, this figure represents an increase of 25 per cent in the four years since the Labour government came to power in 2017, at which time military spending was at $3.27 billion. This is 1.4 per cent of gross domestic product, which is more than countries such as Germany, Canada, Japan and South Africa.[25] When measured per capita, only twenty-two countries have higher military spending than Aotearoa New Zealand's rate of $624.

More importantly, when we look more closely at the allocation of military spending – where the money goes within the NZDF – it serves to highlight the centrality of combat or war-fighting. The budget sections Vote Defence Force and Vote Defence 2021/22 break down the planned military spending into its component parts. The largest proportion of the defence budget ($2.4 billion) goes towards generating capabilities that achieve the levels of readiness for military operations and other tasks as directed by the government of New Zealand. Of this, $990 million is allocated to the Air Force, $870 million to the Army and $500 million to the Navy.[26] Budget documents articulate the intended achievements of this spending, including the capacity for 'maritime warfare operations', 'naval air combat', 'Special Operations Forces' and 'global complex warfighting operations'.

The NZDF also has an extensive asset base and is allocated annual funding for capital expenditure on new assets. This is used for maintaining and obtaining military equipment, much of which supports combat. The NZDF's asset base is worth over $7.5 billion. This includes $3.796 billion in land and buildings and $3.649 billion in specialist military equipment.[27]

While military equipment need not necessarily be combat equipment, and often such equipment could serve both combat and non-combat purposes, the NZDF has proudly advertised the fact that much of its equipment is designed for combat:

> An Army is always among the first to get its hands on the latest technologies. The New Zealand Army is no different. As you would expect, much of the technology at our disposal is designed to help us excel in combat situations.[28]

Indeed, the equipment section of the NZDF's website has a subsection dedicated to 'firepower', which lists models of sniper rifle, mortar, assault rifle, pistol, shotgun, light artillery, grenade launcher, machine gun and shoulder-fired anti-armour weapons that the NZDF utilises.[29] NZDF publications are replete with images of these weapons.

Combat capabilities are a central feature of larger projects, too. The Ministry of Defence's *Major Projects Report 2020* lists nine significant projects that build the NZDF's capabilities across all branches of the military.[30] Two of the three most expensive projects are the purchasing of four P-8A Poseidon aircraft, and systems upgrades to the frigates HMNZS *Te Kaha* and *Te Mana*. So costly is the Poseidon project that its approved budget (more than $2.4 billion) is more than that of the remaining seven projects combined. These remaining projects include, among other things, commissioning multiple naval vessels, replacing the Air Force's fleet of C-130H Hercules, and a helicopter flight simulator for training purposes. The frigate upgrades have an approved budget of around $639 million, while replacing the Hercules aircraft has been allocated about $1.5 billion.

Combat capabilities were an explicit criterion for the acquisition of the Poseidon aircraft and the systems upgrades on *Te Kaha* and *Te Mana*. The *Major Projects Report 2020* lists 'key user requirements' that were considered when assessing how to replace the force's P-3K2 Orion aircraft, which are currently used for air surveillance maritime patrol functions and will be retired by 2025.[31] The ability to carry out anti-submarine and anti-surface warfare are deemed to be two such requirements, requirements that the P-8A Poseidon aircraft meet. Another key criterion was that the systems be interoperable with those of allied militaries due to using the same technologies. As Chief of Defence Force, Kevin Short, said at the time of their purchase:

> We are a military force, and what we wanted for the Government is a response option .... There are plenty of aircraft out there that have a range of endurance and censors [*sic*], but not many have the response. The response being, at some stage, just the mere threat of being able to carry weapons and being able to do something that is aggressive. That allows us to operate at the high ed [*sic*] of the spectrum, which our friends and allies want us to do.[32]

Even if there are no short-term plans to employ this warfare capability, several consequences flow from the decision to possess it. The first and most obvious is cost. Not only are the planes themselves incredibly expensive, but while weaponised they are unable to take off from the Air Force's Whenuapai base, meaning new infrastructure development is required, such as building hangars and strengthening taxiways at the Ohakea base. The Royal New Zealand Air Force Squadron No. 5, which will operate the aircraft, is planning to move from Whenuapai to Ohakea.

In providing this overview of the NZDF – its make-up, funding, equipment and the like – we want to make a number of key points. In the first instance, despite appearances and public perceptions, the NZDF exists for, and is funded and trained primarily for, armed combat. This raises a number of critical questions, such as whether combat preparedness is the right posture for a nation that is not at risk of military invasion, and whether the combat readiness is matched by the number of personnel. Could the NZDF provide credible defence against military invasion by a foreign power or in a major military confrontation in the Pacific, and, if not, are we putting too much effort in terms of training and resources into combat readiness? We must also ask whether combat readiness is the right posture for dealing with other serious security threats, such as the climate crisis, pandemics, cyber-attacks, terrorism and organised crime. Does the training and equipment provided to the NZDF match the kinds of threats and dangers the nation faces in the twenty-first century? Lastly, we have to ask whether the funding and preparation put into combat readiness detracts from the NZDF's ability to engage in other tasks like peacekeeping, humanitarian assistance and disaster relief.

Another key point is that the NZDF receives a large amount of funding, especially in comparison to other nations, but particularly in comparison to other sectors such as health, education, the environment, poverty alleviation and so on. The question is: can spending so much money on combat preparedness really be justified? And what about the opportunity costs of this spending? If the billions spent on the NZDF were put into other areas, might this in fact increase the safety, security and wellbeing of New Zealanders? We will explore these issues further as we proceed in this book.

Finally, an examination of the emphasis the NZDF puts on combat readiness and interoperability raises the underlying question of why this is so. As we saw in the previous section, it is not to stand up an independent territorial defence in the face of potential invasion. Instead, Short's comments provide a clue: operating at the high end of the combat spectrum is what 'our friends and allies want us to do'. Our combat preparedness exists to symbolically support wars being waged by our allies. Shaping New Zealand's military in response to the preferences of countries such as the United States and United Kingdom cements us firmly within the US–Anglo alliance. As we shall see, however, this makes pursuing an independent foreign policy more difficult.

Foreign Policy and the New Zealand Defence Force

The NZDF is a tool of foreign policy because it undertakes a wide range of activities on behalf of Aotearoa in various parts of the globe, some in our Pacific neighbourhood and others in far-flung locations. In a more fundamental sense, though, the NZDF is a tool of foreign policy because the use of a country's military resources is indicative of the international issues that it takes seriously and of which other countries its interests align with. Here, we must remember the historical origins of New Zealand's foreign policy in settler colonialism and British imperialism, its alignment with Britain and its allies, and the way in which continuing cooperation with Anglosphere-led intelligence organisations such as the

Five Eyes network shapes our threat perceptions and international interests. In any event, with the many resources at its disposal, the NZDF is a highly visible and highly active part of New Zealand's foreign policy efforts.[33]

In the previous section, we questioned whether the NZDF is trained, funded and equipped to deal with the range of threats and dangers facing the nation in the twenty-first century. Here, we investigate whether the NZDF supports and advances the independent, values-based foreign policy that many New Zealanders aspire to for Aotearoa. Indeed, could an institution primarily designed for armed combat ever do this effectively? Later chapters will explore these questions in greater detail with regards to the specific activities that the NZDF engages in, namely, peacekeeping, disaster relief and war-fighting. Here, we discuss the ongoing public debate concerning Aotearoa's independent, values-based foreign policy, arguing that what such a policy would entail for the NZDF is often excluded from political debate. We suggest that the NZDF is currently used and deployed in a manner contrary to an independent foreign policy, and we highlight the roadblocks that would exist in reorienting the NZDF to accord with a truly independent policy.

That Aotearoa should have an independent foreign policy is a familiar and popular notion. Past expressions of the idea were seen in Aotearoa's anti-nuclear stance and the anti-apartheid movement, as well as public opposition to the Vietnam War and the 2003 invasion of Iraq. In terms of what such an independent policy might look like now, it is framed by some as delicately distancing ourselves from historic associations with Anglo-American partners in favour of a foreign policy that situates Aotearoa as a Pacific nation concerned with the development and security of the Pacific. For others, this necessarily entails decolonising the foreign policy establishment and processes, and centring Te Tiriti o Waitangi in the formulation and practice of foreign relations.

Renewed popularity of the idea has been driven by several factors, primarily changes in the international system. Internationally, countries such as the United States and United Kingdom have suffered a decrease in status stemming from the failed and unethical twenty-year war on terror, as well as from the rise of right-wing nationalist movements and isolationist policies domestically. Unilateral actions like the United States withdrawing from climate change and arms control agreements, and the United Kingdom leaving the European Union, have further damaged the reputation of these powers as global leaders. At the same time, China has experienced an increase in economic power and signalled its intention to match this with the expansion of its military power. Both the United States and China perceive themselves to be the rightful preeminent power in the Pacific. New Zealand following an independent foreign policy, it is argued, would allow us to navigate a changing international and regional environment, and act as an honest broker between the two superpowers.

It has been questioned whether politicians and those within the military are as keen on this idea as members of the public.[34] At the very least, leaders in each sector clearly feel the need to strike a balance between independence that does not isolate and alliances that do not alienate. There is nothing inherently wrong with this. Most people who would advocate for an independent foreign policy would not disavow all international alliances or engagements and, similarly, many of those who advocate for a strong Anglo-US relationship would not subscribe to unthinkingly following every whim of our more powerful allies. In any case, the notion of an independent foreign policy is so engrained in our national identity that New Zealand governments of whatever political stripe now feel the need to pay at least lip service to promoting an independent foreign policy.[35]

This has continued in recent times. In July 2021, Jacinda Ardern made an address to the New Zealand Institute of International Affairs annual conference. The subject of the conference was Aotearoa's place in the Indo-Pacific region. Some commentators have suggested that the speech was pro-United States, in that the term 'Indo-Pacific' is utilised by representatives of countries such as the United States in order to centralise India in the Asia-Pacific, to the exclusion of China. In any case, Ardern was explicit in identifying the Pacific as New Zealand's place in the world:

> To start – I have a question for you. Where do you see our place in the world? If you were to ask me, I would give you a very literal answer. The Pacific. This is our home. It is the region we most squarely identify with. We very literally share a population base.[36]

Quoting Norman Kirk, Ardern concluded the speech by summarising the notion of an independent, values-based foreign policy as policy that would 'express New Zealand's ideals as well as reflect our national interests'.

Speaking to the same body later that year, Minister of Foreign Affairs, Nanaia Mahuta, spoke of the government's intention to conduct foreign policy in the region via an 'authentic and values-based "Pacific Way"'.[37] These statements are reflected in NZDF publications. The *NZDF Strategic Plan 2019–2025*, for example, states:

> The recognition of operating in the Pacific as equal in priority for the NZDF to New Zealand's own territory is reflective of the Government's Pacific Reset, and the importance of the Pacific to New Zealand's national security.[38]

Presumably, foreign policy that increasingly emphasised New Zealand's role in the Pacific would have material implications for how the NZDF was composed, funded and deployed. But curiously, defence policy – either in relation to the Pacific reset made by the Labour-led government in 2018 or in alternative foreign policy approaches – is not often discussed or articulated by political leaders in public forums. During the 2020 election, for example, the policy.nz website, run by The Spinoff, offered a guide to candidates and their policies. When it came to defence policy, four of the five parties that ended up with seats in Parliament (National, Labour, ACT and Te Pāti Māori) were listed as 'no policies found'. A review of the policy sections of these parties' websites in early 2022 resulted in a similar absence of information about defence policies. While politics in recent times has been dominated by the Covid-19 pandemic, the absence of explicitly articulated policy in an area that receives billions annually is worrisome to say the least.

In early 2023, Te Pāti Māori announced a defence policy based on military neutrality, a core component of which is opposition to New Zealand defence personnel providing military support in overseas operations.[39] The policy was articulated as a matter of sovereignty – as a Māori-centred defence policy that is rangatiratanga and mana motuhake in action. Te Pāti Māori leaders explicitly noted the roots of the policy in the history of discrimination against Māori service personnel and involvement in overseas wars that have not benefited Māori. Co-leader Rawiri Waititi stated, '[t]he time for war, killing and imperialism is over. Now is the time for peace and sovereignty for tangata whenua and indigenous peoples around the world. Aotearoa must be friends to everybody and enemies to nobody.' He went on to emphasise that: 'We will no longer have our sovereignty determined by others, whether it is in Canberra, London, Washington, Beijing or Moscow.'[40]

The one successful party that did have an articulated and publicly available defence and peacekeeping policy in 2020 was the Green Party. (A similar policy document remains on its website.[41]) Prioritising nonviolent means of conflict resolution and international engagement, its key positions include requiring the NZDF to focus its activities within the Pacific region and develop its peacekeeping, humanitarian response and border protection capabilities. The Green policy also contends that 'the roles of the NZDF should not include participation in the ANZUS Treaty, the Five Power Defence Arrangement or the UK/USA intelligence agreement'. Crucially, there is also a recognition that this reorientation of the NZDF would need to be underpinned by how defence funding is spent:

> Expenditure on assets and capabilities for major combat situations should be deprioritised. Aotearoa New Zealand's defence forces should, over time, replace capabilities and assets whose primary function is to enable Aotearoa New Zealand to operate as a subordinate part of a combat task force led by the United States, Britain, or Australia. The nation's focus should turn to maintaining a defence force that concentrates on peacekeeping, disaster relief, and the protection of the nation's maritime borders and resources.[42]

Green Party policy, at least implicitly, seems to recognise that tasks such as humanitarian relief and border/fisheries protection could be (and already partially are) carried out by civilian institutions, and indicates that a review of the NZDF's structure and governance would be required to identify where the responsibilities of civilian entities would end and where the remit of the NZDF would begin. While this is an important perspective to add to political discussions, we would argue that it does not go far enough. The Green Party does not offer any justification as to why the NZDF is required at all, given its inability to provide adequate defence against invasion, its excessive costs, its primary focus on combat readiness and its unsuitability to responding to current threats and dangers.

In contrast, while keeping a defence force, Te Pāti Māori's plan would reorient it as a 'support force for the Pacific, for our Polynesian world'.[43] This force would respond to civil defence emergencies, according to Debbie Ngarewa-Packer. Much of what Te Pāti Māori has proposed aligns with the argument for change we will present in Chapter 4. We certainly think the reformulation of the NZDF to concentrate on regional matters such as response to civil emergencies is viable and preferrable to the status quo. This would require huge changes to the NZDF, given the recent history of overseas war-fighting, and related patterns of military spending, discussed above.

Turning to a more empirical and historical perspective, we can chart how closely NZDF operations have aligned with the government's foreign policy objectives by glancing at a map of NZDF deployments in the past few decades. Here we can see that the preponderance of deployments in the Middle East seems to be aligned with the counter-terrorism agenda that has been pursued by the US–Anglo alliance in the past twenty years. In the NZDF's 2021 annual report, ten of the thirteen operations, or contributions to operations, listed in the 'Military Operations in Support of a Rules-Based International Order' section of the report were occurring in the Middle East and environs.[44] Two of the remaining three relate to imposing sanctions upon

North Korea and maintaining the demilitarised zone between South Korea and North Korea. One of these is based in South Korea, the other in Japan. The final operation is based in South Sudan.

Two of the operations in the Middle East would be thought of as traditional peacekeeping operations. One is a contribution to the United Nations Truce Supervision Organization, which has a mission to help preserve peace between Israel and neighbouring states. The other is a contribution to the Multinational Force and Observers, a non-UN peacekeeping mission monitoring the peace treaty between Egypt and Israel on the Sinai Peninsula.

From what can be discerned about the remaining eight deployments taking place in the wider Middle East, all concerned combating terrorism. The training of local military counterparts was under way at the time in Afghanistan (Operation RUA II), while two separate operations, MOHUA and KERERU, stationing personnel in Iraq, Kuwait and Qatar, were listed as contributions to the Global Coalition to Defeat the Islamic State of Iraq and Syria (ISIS). Operation PUKEKO was contributing to the Combined Maritime Forces based in Bahrain, which declares the defeat of terrorism to be one of its main goals.[45]

In Jordan, under a redacted operation name, the NZDF is also contributing to the multinational Operation Gallant Phoenix. Gallant Phoenix is an intelligence-sharing operation that 'enhances the ability of member nations to understand and respond to current, evolving and future violent extremist threats'.[46] In all of these operations, Aotearoa New Zealand works in close

Table 1: Ongoing Deployments as of 2020 Briefing to the Incoming Minister of Defence

OPERATION NAME	LOCATION	DESCRIPTION
RUA II	Afghanistan	Contribution to the NATO Resolute Support Mission.
PUKEKO	Bahrain	Provision of command and specialist support to coalition maritime security operations at the Combined Maritime Forces Headquarters.
FARAD	Egypt	Deployment to the Multinational Force and Observers, Sinai Peninsula, Egypt, supervising the peace treaty between Egypt and Israel.
MOHUA	Iraq and Kuwait	Deployment to the United States-led Operation Inherent Resolve in Iraq and Kuwait. Part of New Zealand's contribution to the Defeat ISIS Coalition.
SCORIA	Golan Heights and Lebanon	Deployment to the United Nations Truce Supervision Organization, monitoring the truce agreements between Israel and Syria, and Israel and Lebanon.
MONITOR	Republic of Korea	Contribution of personnel to the United Nations Command Military Armistice Commission, which monitors and supports the implementation of the armistice agreement signed at the end of the Korean War, plus contribution to the US-led United Nations Command Headquarters.
[Redacted name]	Jordan	Contribution of personnel to New Zealand's multi-agency contribution to Operation Gallant Phoenix, a platform for collection, monitoring and sharing of material regarding potential and existing domestic and global threats.
SUDDEN	South Sudan	Peace support deployment to the United Nations Mission in South Sudan.
WHIO	Japan	Maritime surveillance deployments in support of United Nations Security Council sanctions against North Korea.
KERERU	Qatar	NZDF personnel to the US Combined Air Operations Centre in Qatar as a part of New Zealand's contribution to the Defeat ISIS Coalition.

collaboration with members of the US–Anglo alliance. Ninety-three personnel were deployed around the world at the time of the incoming Minister of Defence's 2020 briefing.[47]

That figure excludes the major deployments to the Middle East that have taken place in recent years and thus minimises the concentration of the NZDF's work there. For example, between 2015 and 2020, in response to ISIS's capture of large amounts of territory in Iraq and Syria, NZDF personnel were deployed to assist with training members of the Iraqi security forces (Operation MANAWA). Close to 150 NZDF were deployed at any one time during the height of this operation. Similarly, while in 2020 Operation RUA II (which concluded in early 2021), mentioned above, had a mandated size of only thirteen personnel, the NZDF's near twenty-year deployment to Afghanistan involved more than 3,500 personnel, ten of whom lost their lives, and as of 2013, when the number of personnel deployed was substantially decreased, had cost around $300 million.[48]

In contrast to operations in the Middle East, many NZDF activities in the Asia-Pacific region are relatively small, brief and ad hoc. Operations defined as 'military operations in support of a rules-based international order' were allocated around sixty times more funding in the 2021/22 Budget than those defined as 'military operations that contribute to regional security'.[49] The latter category includes activities in the Asia-Pacific region, such as humanitarian assistance to Indonesia in late 2018 following the tsunami at Palu, and Operation MOA, which provided logistics support to the Solomon Islands' national election process.[50] The Mutual Assistance Programme, an 'integral component of NZ's contribution to peace and security in the Asia Pacific', appears to include only eight NZDF members assigned to permanent roles in Pacific nations.[51]

We do not wish to diminish the valuable work that the NZDF has done in the Pacific in terms of either humanitarian assistance or peacekeeping. Humanitarian relief efforts carried out by the NZDF, such as that provided to Tonga following the January 2022 volcanic eruption, are of vital importance to the wellbeing of people in the region. One of the most notable examples of such work was the NZDF's response to Cyclone Winston in 2016: 'One of New Zealand's biggest peacetime deployments to the Pacific, the Fiji operation included 500 defence staff, two ships and six aircraft.'[52] More recently, the NZDF has assisted Pacific nations such as Papua New Guinea in their response to Covid-19, transporting much needed medical supplies. Operations such as this clearly make an important contribution to the security and wellbeing of people in the region. At the same time, New Zealand's colonial history in the region should not be forgotten. The precursors to the NZDF historically played a central role in maintaining colonial relations in the region, and New Zealand's relationships with some Pacific states remain problematic as a consequence of this history.

Nevertheless, these recent deployments, both in disaster relief and peacekeeping operations, illustrate the valuable role that Aotearoa has played, and can continue to play, in the Pacific – although this needs to occur in ways that contribute to decolonisation and Treaty partnership. They also demonstrate that much of this good was achieved by nonviolent, non-military means, even in cases of extreme violence, such as in Bougainville in the late 1990s (discussed below), and thus raise the question of whether a combat-ready military force is a requirement for an independent, values-based role in the Pacific. We will discuss this further in later chapters. For now, the point is that it is precisely because Aotearoa has a demonstrated history of being able to do some good in the Pacific, notwithstanding its role during the central colonial period, that we contend that more of its foreign affairs and defence policy should be oriented towards doing so.

Some might ask whether we can have our cake and eat it, too. Can we have an independent, values-based foreign policy, one in which we might emphasise being a good Pacific neighbour, while also being a stalwart ally of the United States and other traditional Anglosphere powers? More specifically, can the NZDF serve as a tool for achieving both? We believe that Aotearoa New Zealand cannot excel to the best of its abilities at one while also fulfilling the other. Moreover, the institutional make-up, training and equipping of the NZDF prohibits Aotearoa from fully committing to the independent course.

As an example, let's return to the purchase of the Poseidon aircraft discussed above. As noted, a key issue in the decision is interoperability, a core component of the NZDF's strategic planning:

> Whether at home or abroad, the Defence Force will most likely be operating alongside other Government agencies and New Zealand's international partners.

The Defence Force must therefore maintain capabilities that enable it to work effectively with others, notably Australia and the Five Eyes nations. This interoperability amplifies the Defence Force's ability to contribute to multinational operations and facilitates integration with partners' capabilities .... Interoperability with our traditional partners is a critical strategic imperative for the Defence Force.[53]

Crucially, the references to the Five Eyes network and 'traditional partners' makes it clear that interoperability is largely viewed in terms of the US–Anglo alliance.

In other words, the military capabilities that New Zealand purchases are determined by, and in turn, determine, who Aotearoa aligns itself with. These technologies are not neutral tools. Rather, the states that we will be most able to act in concert with are literally *built into* the technologies we procure. This is how the relationships materially shape risk assessments and interests, and it is particularly true of combat-specific capabilities, due to the lengths that nations go in order to ensure that adversaries are not familiar with their weapons systems. Finally, the drive for interoperability means that large sums of money will continue to be spent to enable New Zealand to collaborate with our closest allies:

Advances in technology and the military capabilities being brought into service by Defence partners will have significant interoperability implications for New Zealand's decisions around Defence capabilities. In general, keeping in line with New Zealand's partners will increasingly require more sophisticated platforms and enabling infrastructure.[54]

The second issue, also seen in the example of the Poseidon aircraft and related to that of interoperability, is that capabilities that can in theory serve both combat or civilian purposes, such as search and rescue operations, will always be torn between the two. Reporting on the work of Squadron 5, the squadron that will crew the Poseidon aircraft, has highlighted that even prior to the purchase of these new aircraft, much of the squadron's work was taking place in the Middle East:

> About a tenth of Squadron 5's hours are currently dedicated to search and rescue operations, while patrolling fisheries and customs in New Zealand waters and the South Pacific accounts for about a quarter to a third of its time .... The squad's international output – like the joint counter-piracy work in the Middle East – accounts for about half of their flying hours, and about a third of the hours go into training.[55]

Indeed, this point has been made with reference to the NZDF's resources more generally in civil defence planning. The National Civil Defence Emergency Management Plan Order 2015 notes that 'the New Zealand Defence Force cannot guarantee that certain resources will always be available [for disaster relief], because they may be involved in another Government-directed mission'.[56] In other words, the composition, training, equipment and funding of the NZDF limits its use as a tool for working towards greater security and wellbeing in the Pacific, or even responding to natural disasters domestically, and instead pushes it towards working with its powerful allies in combat-related roles. This clearly limits its role in the promotion of an independent, values-based foreign policy, particularly given the involvement of the NZDF in operations associated with the global war on terror in recent years.

The New Zealand Defence Force and National Collective Memory

Throughout the course of this book, we suggest that abolishing the NZDF in favour of other security approaches is a rational or logical course of action given, among other things, the cost of maintaining the NZDF, the NZDF's inability to defend Aotearoa's territorial sovereignty or deal with contemporary threats, the marginal contribution the NZDF makes to an independent, values-based, decolonised foreign policy and, as we will show, the failure of armed violence more generally to establish international stability, peace and democracy. We might like to think that policy in an area as important as national defence is governed by a thorough analysis of relevant information and arguments, but in actuality militaries maintain their place and value in society, at least in part, for reasons connected to rather slippery concepts, such as collective memory and national identity.

Collective memory is 'a form of memory that is shared by a group and of central importance to the social identity of the group's members'.[57] These memories can be seen as shared understandings about the past of a collective. The *collective* in 'collective memory' can apply to many social units, from families to the members of certain institutions such as schools or sports teams. However, collective memory is most often discussed in the context of the nation-state. Indeed, early explorations of the concept of nationalism noted how processes of remembering and forgetting are essential to the formation of a nation. As nineteenth-century French scholar Ernest Renan, discussing the formation of the French nation-state, noted: 'Forgetting ... is a crucial factor in the creation of a nation, which is why progress in historical studies often constitutes a danger to nationality'.[58] He likens such forgetfulness to falling into 'historical error'. There are two important points to take from Renan's assertion. First, the existence of a nation and its national identity requires memories that are shared by, and important to, the members of that nation. Second, these memories are not randomly acquired but are the product of selective attention to history.

Renan used the example of France and French monarchs, but the political nature of collective memory can also be clearly seen in Aotearoa New Zealand's history. Vincent O'Malley's work on the New Zealand Wars shows how these conflicts have been obscured in retellings of Aotearoa New Zealand's history. O'Malley argues that the practice of 'forgetting' these colonial conflicts stems from the fact that they were a source of discomfort for many Pākehā, and because acknowledging this history serves to problematise the notion that Aotearoa New Zealand has a history of positive race relations.[59] From this perspective, it is not surprising that the historic role played by precursors to the NZDF in the violent suppression of Māori and the maintenance of Pākehā power, and the differential treatment of Māori service personnel (such as exclusion from post-war assistance or honours), has been obscured and replaced by the positive Anzac myth.

While internal conflict is often excluded from a nation's collective memory, conversely, wars in which a nation is depicted as unifying to fight an Other are often focal points for national identity. (We say 'depicted' as this representation can be true or false to varying degrees.) As political scientist and historian Benedict Anderson states: 'No more arresting emblems of the modern culture of nationalism exist than cenotaphs and tombs of Unknown Soldiers . . . void as these tombs are of identifiable mortal remains or immortal souls, they are nonetheless saturated with ghostly national imaginings.'[60]

New Zealand is no exception. The notion that New Zealand was born as a distinct nation during World War I, and in the fighting at Gallipoli in particular, has been prominent. John Bevan-Smith has compiled several instances in which journalists, historians and politicians discussed this perspective, including the following:[61]

> During the war itself many New Zealanders came to believe that the performance of the soldiers on foreign fields had established the country's 'manhood' in the eyes of the world. The war was considered the birth of national identity. At welcome-home receptions, and in

Anzac Day speeches, the Kiwi soldier was praised for his physique, his courage, his ingenuity – and the plaudits of foreign observers were endlessly rehearsed.[62]

Our national commemorations of New Zealand's role in past wars often reify these notions. For example, Prime Minister Jim Bolger suggested in 1996 that Anzac Day should be a day not only of commemoration but also a celebration of our nationhood.[63]

This understanding of Aotearoa's history is problematic for a raft of reasons, but the key point for our argument is that, for some, the NZDF is valuable not only in what it does, but in what it symbolically represents. It is a symbol of the birth of New Zealand, the country's ascendance to the world stage and the courage shown by its soldiers. Abolishing the NZDF would be confronting for many New Zealanders and therefore a damaging policy position for any political party to take. This perhaps explains the lack of real political debate concerning defence policy which we have noted.

The enduring salience of our national creation myth can be seen, for example, in John Key's consideration in 2014 of a badged ANZAC deployment to Iraq. Key admitted that such an approach would limit New Zealand's control of its troops (a central operational matter), but nevertheless entertained the notion for its symbolic value.[64] The final deployment – ultimately not badged under ANZAC – was opposed by all parties but National and ACT.

Summary

In this chapter, we have explored the historical origins, financial cost, composition, training, equipment and deployments of the NZDF. Many New Zealanders perceive the NZDF to be a capable, security-directed and values-driven organisation that is oriented towards roles like humanitarian assistance and peacekeeping – this is what we call the myth of the NZDF. Our assessment suggests a different reality. The NZDF is in fact anachronistic, not least because it has its roots in colonial conquest and imperial support. Today, the NZDF is funded, equipped and trained primarily for armed combat, often in direct support of the Anglosphere, despite the government's own assessment that the chances of a direct threat to Aotearoa's territory are extremely low and the NZDF is too small to defend Aotearoa in such circumstances. Its composition, training and equipment mean that it is geared towards interoperability with its powerful allies, which in turn contradicts the role many perceive it to have in promoting an independent, values-driven, Pacific-oriented foreign policy. The very expensive NZDF's primary function is to fight with its more powerful allies and act as a unifying symbol of New Zealand national identity (despite its precursor's historic role in the New Zealand Wars). We suggest that these contradictions between myth and reality ought to be up for sustained public debate. With the New Zealand public's dissonant views of the NZDF understood and acknowledged, we will be in a better position to consider alternatives.

2. The Myth of National Security

What exactly is security, and how is it best achieved? During the Cold War, and particularly in the immediate aftermath of the Second World War, which caused so much devastation across the world, most people believed that having a strong military which could defend against an invasion of the nation's territory, or possessing powerful weapons that could deter hostile states, or perhaps belonging to a powerful alliance that could provide mutual protection, were the best guarantees of national security. In other words, influenced by the events of World War II and the subsequent Cold War, it was widely agreed that security primarily entails protection from external military threats.

Since then, however, scholars have been studying the nature of security and have come to realise that security is defined both by values and perceptions and by a broad contextual range of potential risks and dangers.[1] In turn, these chosen values and perceived threats determine the strategies a nation will adopt to keep itself secure. A state like Switzerland, for example, despite being in the middle of a historically volatile region, highly values its independence and thus chooses strict neutrality and a low level of military preparedness to avoid getting drawn into a conflict. Other states in Europe, by contrast, have chosen to develop independent nuclear weapons (France) or join military alliances such as the North Atlantic Treaty Organization (NATO) (Germany) to try to guarantee their security. The key point is that there are different perceptions and values of security, and a nation's identity and perceived interests will determine how it goes about the business of securing itself. There is no one way or right way to pursue national security.

On the other hand, many nations, as well as scholars, have come to realise that if security means freedom from threats and dangers and the ability of a nation to pursue its way of life without interference or disruptions, then we need to consider other kinds of risks and dangers apart from the threat of military invasion.[2] The Covid-19 pandemic, for example, has killed, as of mid-2023, almost seven million people globally, seriously damaged the global economy and forced significant disruptive changes to the way people work and live.[3] In this sense, it is a major security issue – it not only harms people and their means of survival, but interferes with a nation's way of life. The climate crisis, organised crime, disinformation and conspiracy theories, and violent extremism can all have similar kinds of effects. For this reason, some security studies scholars have suggested that we need to consider security in broader sectoral terms and think closely about not just military security, but also economic security, environmental security, cultural security, energy security, food security and so on.

Tying many of these concerns together is the concept of 'human security'. This idea encompasses many of the forms of security noted above, because it goes beyond mere survival or military security to include any threat or risk that can inhibit the wellbeing and flourishing of humans, their societies, their support systems and their environment. Some scholars have defined human security as 'survival *plus*', where the 'plus' refers to people being free 'from life-determining threats, and therefore [having] space to make choices'.[4] This conception suggests that security means more than just protection from military attacks (though we will cover this later); it also includes things like access to the means of life, to healthcare and education, to a healthy environment, to cultural expression and identity, to social support and to help when needed, such as in the case of natural disasters.

Thinking of security in this holistic way can be compared to the movement by governments around the world to start assessing budgetary policy by how it affects people's wellbeing rather than economic measures of national growth alone. Just as national economic growth might seem hollow in cases where growing inequality leads to citizens sharing unequally in the outcomes of economic productivity, so too might 'security' in a country that is safe from foreign aggression or interference but in which people's agency and safety is inhibited by poverty, crime, lack of healthcare, structural racism, political repression or environmental degradation. With its nuclear weapons and powerful military, North Korea is arguably secure from foreign invasion, but its citizens are far from secure by most other measures. Indeed, the Ministry of Defence's *Defence White Paper 2016*, while using the language of national security, acknowledged that 'security is the condition which permits New Zealand citizens to go about their daily business confidently, free from fear and able to make the most of opportunities to advance their way of life'.[5]

Framing security in a broader way helps to identify and prioritise the range of different threats that New Zealanders face, highlighting that many of these are non-military in nature. This is not merely a conceptual exercise. Rather, even if for the moment we narrow our focus to exclude domestic matters such as the cost of living or rates of domestic violence and instead concentrate on the international and transnational security environment, in the dynamic global and Pacific context many of the dangers that confront Aotearoa are not limited to the kinds of traditional military threats that characterised the post-war and Cold War periods. Instead, these new threats align well with the notion of human security.

In this chapter, we expand on some of the issues raised in the previous chapter and explore the outdated security myth which underpins the approaches and deployments of the New Zealand Defence Force, as well as the true nature of the current threats and dangers facing Aotearoa. The aim is to assess whether the security definition and approach we have adopted, and the means we rely on to create security, match up with or make sense in the current environment. Our assessment is that Aotearoa's national security approach, with its reliance on the NZDF and military cooperation with the Anglosphere powers, is anachronistic and more of a legacy of a bygone era than an accurate reflection of present global realities. Consequently, we would be better off if we reformulated our broader approach to security and abolished the NZDF.

The Changing Military Threatscape

Before we examine the way in which broader, non-military, threats and dangers have come to define the threat environment, let's examine the current military threatscape. As is well known, in response to the 9/11 terrorist attacks, US President George W. Bush launched what became known as the 'global war on terror' (GWOT). Many of the armed conflicts that are either part of the GWOT or which began concurrently differ somewhat from most wars of the twentieth century. The nature of the 9/11 attacks not only elevated terrorism to the top of governments' foreign and security policy concerns, but also exacerbated already changing trends in armed conflict globally.

For example, as major research projects such as the Uppsala Conflict Data Program have demonstrated, the number of interstate wars – full-scale military conflicts between sovereign states, such as the Russian invasion of Ukraine – had been declining significantly since the end of the Cold War.[6] At the same time, the number of intrastate wars – violent political conflicts within states between groups and factions – had been greatly increasing. Today, with only a few exceptions (such as the war between Russia and Ukraine), the vast majority of military conflicts in the world are within states or involve non-traditional military conflict involving non-state actors like terrorists, insurgents or criminal organisations (such as the drug cartels in Mexico). An important feature of these contemporary intrastate wars is that many of them are internationalised in the sense that one or more external states have intervened militarily in support of one side to the conflict. The wars in Afghanistan, Iraq, Somalia, Yemen and Syria are all examples of these types of internationalised internal conflicts, as is the war in the Democratic Republic of Congo. In each case, neighbouring states, or foreign powers further afield, sometimes with a neocolonial agenda, are deeply involved in the conflict, providing military assistance and support to one or more factions.

Importantly, internationalised intrastate wars are characterised by asymmetric combat in which the military resources of one party or bloc of parties are often dramatically smaller than those of their opponents. This partly explains the prevalence of insurgency, guerrilla or terrorist tactics in modern warfare, as less-well-resourced groups seek to avoid direct large-scale engagement with adversaries. This, in turn, helps to explain the counter-insurgency tactics employed by states such as the United States and United Kingdom when participating in these types of conflicts. The practice of torture and detention, the employment of mercenary forces, the use of automated weapons such as drones, the increased reliance on special forces and intelligence-gathering activities, while having historic precedents (such as during the colonial and Cold War periods), are often justified on the basis that terrorist or rebel groups are impossible to defeat via more traditional military tactics.

This kind of unconventional, hybrid warfare in which large-scale military confrontations are rare, and usually non-decisive when they do occur, is now the norm when it comes to military conflict. Even in cases of conventional interstate war, such as the current Russia–Ukraine war, it can be seen that insurgency tactics and the use of drones, small arms and artillery, as well as the role of information and intelligence, are proving more decisive than the large-scale military hardware and tactics of the past, such as the mass deployment of tanks, ships and airpower. In other words, the nature of military conflict has changed dramatically in the last few decades, and with the spread of light weapons and robotic and information technology, not to mention the impact of climate change on vulnerable societies, will no doubt continue to evolve further.

The conflicts of the present and future will most likely continue to entail hybrid forms of activities carried out by military forces, including community policing, infrastructure security and civilian protection, information management, peacekeeping, humanitarian and development assistance, and many other complex tasks. Moreover, they will necessarily involve task-sharing and coordination with a range of civilian actors, and there will be no clear moment of 'victory', but a more gradual transition to another state of cold conflict or peace. As we have seen in Afghanistan, Iraq, Syria and elsewhere, it is unlikely that any side will be able to claim that they have decisively won or settled the conflict.

For more than twenty years, the GWOT has been the dominant military threatscape both globally and from a New Zealand perspective. As discussed above and in more detail below, the greatest number of, longest and most heavily resourced deployments of the NZDF in recent times have pertained to the GWOT. It is both representative of the current state of armed conflict globally and reflects longstanding trends. Using a threshold of 1,000 or more battle-related deaths per year, the Peace Research Institute Oslo (PRIO) determined there to be six armed conflicts serious enough to be considered wars in 2018.[7] These six wars were all in some way linked to the broader GWOT, were taking place in four countries (Yemen, Somalia, Syria and Afghanistan), and accounted for 82 per cent of all recorded battle-related deaths globally in 2018.[8] In 2019, seven conflicts could be classified as wars; in 2020 the number had increased to eight. PRIO notes that 2020 was 'dominated by many of the same conflicts that were present 30 years ago', with the eight wars occurring in seven countries: Afghanistan, Yemen, Somalia, Nigeria, Azerbaijan, Syria and Ethiopia.[9]

While some scholars are beginning to debate whether the main phase of the GWOT is over, its infrastructure – the laws, the counter-terrorism agencies, the spending, the surveillance systems, the banking regulations, the security measures, the training programmes, the military bases, Guantanamo Bay, and the continued public rhetoric and media coverage – is still in place, and GWOT-style conflicts are still the most common globally. These are internationalised intrastate wars, the deadliest conflicts, and of most concern to the US–Anglo alliance. In other words, conflicts similar to those included within the GWOT are what Aotearoa New Zealand is most likely to be called on to participate in for the foreseeable future.

A serious set of questions needs to be asked about whether conventional military training and force composition, and equipment designed for traditional interstate wars are still relevant. We contend that the NZDF, particularly in terms of its large-scale military equipment and its focus on force interoperability with the United States and United Kingdom, is not really relevant for the main types of military conflicts that exist today, nor even for the kinds of interstate wars which could occur. However, reorienting the NZDF to fight these unconventional, unresolvable wars is also pointless. An entirely new approach and paradigm will be required to deal with the threat of contemporary hybrid warfare and the other dangers facing Aotearoa.

The Failures of Military Force

The limitations of military force and the NZDF go deeper than simply a failure to adapt to the changing nature of warfare and types of military conflict that dominate the global environment today. There are, in fact, compelling reasons to doubt that the use of military force, or any kind of state violence, is useful or effective at all as a tool of security or state policy. This may be a confronting notion for many people – we are culturally conditioned to believe that states employ military force because it is a rational, necessary and effective tool of statecraft. In other words, to most people it is no more than common sense that violence requires some kind of opposing violence or force in response, and threats of violence require similar counter-threats.

Interestingly, and in opposition to the popular viewpoint, scholars have recently started to gain a more realistic understanding of the nature, consequences and limits of employing military force as a tool of policy through a series of rigorous empirical studies. What they have found is that the use of military force or violence rarely works to achieve its aims, and there is 'gathering evidence for the ineffectiveness of violence in a variety of empirical literatures'.[10] For example, there is evidence that the states with the greatest capabilities in material and military terms are no more likely to win wars than states with weaker capabilities and, in the past few decades, these strong states are winning wars less often than in previous centuries.[11] Consequently, this is reducing the deterrent power of militaries, and making military power less effective as a tool in foreign policy.

The idea makes sense of why the United States, the greatest military superpower the world has ever seen, failed to win wars in Vietnam, Somalia, Iraq and, most recently, Afghanistan, and why the United Kingdom and France lost wars against much weaker opponents in places like Indochina, Malaya and Algeria. It also explains why Russia has found it so difficult to prevail against its much weaker neighbour, Ukraine, in recent times, and why it lost in Afghanistan in the 1980s after nearly a decade of fighting. In fact, it is difficult to find many cases at all where states have decisively won wars in the last few decades. Even where a clear-cut military victory was achieved, it rarely translated into longer-term political or strategic gains.

Related to this, studies show that when states use military force and violent repression to try to suppress popular protest, it too rarely works.[12] There is even evidence to show that the use of military force or violence to try to protect civilians at risk of armed groups in situations of war or repression rarely works.[13] In many instances, the use of military force to protect civilians can lead to *higher* numbers of civilian casualties as they get caught up in the fighting.[14] Similar limitations have been found about the use of force in counter-terrorism: when states rely on military force to try to deter or counter terrorist attacks, it most often doesn't work or makes the situation worse.[15] In particular, the use of torture and drone assassination as a means of preventing terrorism has been shown to be ineffective at best, and counter-productive at worst.[16] Since 9/11, despite the launch of major counter-terrorist operations in Afghanistan, Iraq, Syria, Pakistan, Somalia and elsewhere – the global war on terror, in other words – the number of terrorist groups and violent attacks has actually increased.

On the other side of the ledger, there is also empirical evidence to demonstrate that non-state use of violence against the state in the form of terrorism or armed insurgencies is also rarely effective.[17] In fact, the use of military violence or force on either side has been shown to be a strong predictor of future episodes of political violence.[18] The use of military force, in other words, instead of leading to peace, stability and security, most often appears to create many of the necessary conditions for further outbreaks of violence. Certainly, if we contemplate the recent historical record of military force – in places like Korea, Palestine, Colombia, Vietnam, Somalia, Ethiopia, Afghanistan, Iraq and Libya, among many others – we have to acknowledge how rarely it leads to peace and security, how unpredictable its results can be (such as the rise of ISIS in Iraq), and how the use of military force and the achievement of political or strategic goals bears no direct relation.[19] The failures of the NZDF in conflicts like Gallipoli, Vietnam and Afghanistan would appear to confirm this pattern, and as we have already noted there is little question that the NZDF would be unsuccessful in defending Aotearoa's territory from invasion at a minimum.

Crucially, there are a number of obvious reasons why violence and military force fail and are so limited in their ability to provide lasting peace and security. Without going into detail, we can note that most people, including policymakers, misunderstand and confuse the relation-ship between the use of brute force and the ability to coerce, control or deter an opponent.[20] This is because the effectiveness of violence in deterring or compelling others depends entirely on how people respond to the threat or use of violence, which cannot be influenced by the violence itself. The ability to hurt and destroy actually has little relationship to the ability to coerce and compel.[21] In fact, the use of violence or force can provoke a variety of responses in the intended target, including deterrence or retaliation, intimidation or rage, submission or resistance, and the expected response can never be guaranteed.[22] This explains why the reliability of military force as a tool of policy is so often mistaken, and why there are so many cases of unexpected or unforeseen consequences. As one scholar puts it:

> [Hannah] Arendt's theory of action demonstrates that violence is not as reliable as is often assumed. Killing people does not have predictable political results because it operates in the 'somewhat intangible' '"web" of human relations' which makes it difficult to know what meanings people will assign to it or what actions they will take in response to it.[23]

Directly related to this, people also misunderstand the relationship between power and military force or violence. The reality is that they don't really have anything to do with each other, because the use of force or violence is a unilateral action by one actor against another, while power involves a *relationship* of subordination. What this means is that the most extreme outcome of violence – the death of the other person – results in the end of any relationship and of any subordination. In other words, killing effectively destroys power because it ends the relationship.[24] As Arendt puts it, 'power and violence are opposites; where the one rules absolutely, the other is absent . . . . Violence can destroy power; it is utterly incapable of creating it.'[25] The key point here is that the view that nations require strong military force in order to wield power is mistaken at best, and the pursuit of military capabilities as an enhancement of national power is fruitless.

A final reason why military force fails so often and so spectacularly is because, despite prevalent views, it is not, and can never be, simply a *tool* of policy. Rather, military force is what social scientists call *constitutive*. That is, it cannot be employed like a surgeon who uses a scalpel in surgery and leaves it in the theatre as she goes home. Instead, the use of military violence and force changes the nation that employs it; there is an inexorable connection between means and ends. In large part, this is because in order to use military force, a society has to build weapons, train people to kill, develop ethical rules which sanction killing, maintain categories of friends and enemies and those who can be killed without compunction, and provide cultural practices which provide meaning to those who lose their lives in war. All of these things leave their mark on a society; at the very least, they embed a widespread belief that war is sometimes necessary and justifiable, and that the military exists for a good reason and ought to be respected. Importantly, involvement in violence can help to create a sense of national identity, such as Aotearoa's belief that its national identity was created at Gallipoli and that New Zealanders are a nation of good global citizens who are always willing to fight for their mates.

In addition, given that violence often produces unexpected outcomes, as we have noted, and given that it is constitutive or reality-making, it can be argued that military force changes the world whenever it is used. At the very least, all of those who suffer from violence are left with physical and/or psychological wounds and a sense of grievance, sometimes which can provoke future violent retaliation. If we consider the violent intervention by Western powers in the Middle East over the past hundred years, for example, we can see that the long-term consequence of this is a deep sense of grievance that has led to numerous terrorist attacks, including those of 9/11. Even when violence is employed in an ostensibly good cause, such as to try to protect a group of innocent people who are being threatened, it's likely that such an action will, in the long term, reinforce the conditions and processes that encourage future resorts to violence. This could lead to the entrenchment of an ongoing cycle of violence and the perpetuation of innocent suffering. It's for this reason that Mahatma Gandhi made the well-known assertion: 'I object to violence because when it appears to do good, the good is only temporary; the evil it does is permanent.'[26] Arendt made a similar observation: 'The practice of violence, like all action, changes the world, but the most probable change is to a more violent world.'[27]

The employment of military force in world politics is regulated by what has historically been called Just War Theory (JWT). This theory, which is now embedded in international law, says that states may only use force under a set of strict conditions, including: that it is the final resort after all other peaceful avenues have been honestly tried and failed; that it is only for defensive purposes or to protect the innocent; that it is authorised by a proper authority; that it is conducted in ways that minimise the suffering of innocent civilians; that it has a high probability of success; and that the outcomes of the violence will result in less suffering and harm than allowing the threat to continue. With the changing nature of warfare in which interstate wars are now infrequent, the often unpredictable outcomes of military violence, its world-changing consequences for the societies that employ it and its inherent unreliability and frequent lack of success, we believe that just wars are rarely possible.[28] (The current Ukraine war may be one, as was World War II in its time.) Certainly, there are real questions to be asked about whether any of the wars of the past few decades would meet a strict interpretation of JWT, especially when we take into account the civilian casualties, the use of torture, the lack of clear success and, importantly, the lack of real efforts to find peaceful alternatives to war.

To give this discussion some empirical grounding, we should consider the example of the many failures and dubious ethics of the use of military force in the GWOT. The use of military violence has become the central approach of many states in their attempt to respond to acts of terrorism, most notably the major Anglosphere states, and we now have more than twenty years of evidence by which to assess this approach. In the first instance, the human cost of the GWOT has been extraordinary, with far more civilians killed in counter-terrorism operations than were killed in the 9/11 attacks or subsequent terrorist attacks. The Watson Institute for International and Public Affairs at Brown University reports that by September 2022, 176,000 people had been killed in the war in Afghanistan since 2001. Of those, 46,000 were civilians.[29] By the same date, 306,000 civilians had been killed since the 2003 invasion of Iraq. These figures exclude deaths indirectly linked to the violence in those countries via malnutrition, diminished healthcare or similar circumstances accompanying the conflicts. When this appraisal is extended to other countries affected by the GWOT, and when the millions of people displaced and harmed in other ways by the violence and insecurity are included, the impact can be seen as even greater. One estimate put the death toll of the GWOT since 2001 at more than a million.[30]

As well as having these human consequences, the GWOT's employment of military violence has been ineffective in its main aims. Far from being defeated, terrorist groups and terrorist attacks have increased globally since 2001. Indeed, not only have military responses to terrorism, such as the invasions of Afghanistan and Iraq, failed to stop terrorist violence, they have been associated with increased terrorist attacks. In part, this is because military invasion and occupation, and the inevitable suffering inflicted on civilian populations as a result, provides fertile ground for terrorist recruitment. The creation of ISIS is one example of this. Furthermore, the GWOT has failed to bring about democracy or increased freedom in the Middle East, as noted by the Freedom House report in 2020, but has instead contributed to increased political instability and insecurity.[31] Indeed, many countries affected by the GWOT, such as Syria, Yemen, and Somalia, are considered some of the 'least free' nations on earth. This is a clear illustration of the failure of military force to achieve either strategic or political goals.

Those who support the GWOT, and Aotearoa New Zealand's participation in it, often claim that it is necessary to uphold a rules-based, liberal international order. That is to say, the defeat of terrorism and authoritarianism is required for the maintenance of international law, as terrorists and despots don't play by the rules. As cited earlier, the NZDF says its various operations in the Middle East are conducted 'in support of a rules-based international order'. However, the GWOT has in many ways resulted in the direct opposite of this goal, undermining and degrading many of the norms of governance and international relations. This is the result of the illegal preemptive invasion of Iraq without United Nations authorisation, the use of illegal practices like torture, extraordinary rendition and drone assassination, and the cynical use of the terrorism threat to increase state surveillance, restrict civil liberties, repress minority groups and generally erode human rights protections.[32]

Other effects of the GWOT include the intensification of Islamophobia, xenophobia, white supremacist ideologies and right-wing nationalism. In the years after 9/11, the Islamist motivations of terrorists were heavily overstated. Our World in Data, based at the University of Oxford, reports that in the United States between 2006 and 2015 terrorist attacks in which the perpetrator was Muslim had, on average, 357 per cent more news articles produced about the attack than cases in which the perpetrator was not Muslim. Yet in this same period only 12.5 per cent of terrorist attacks in the United States were perpetrated by Muslims.[33]

More broadly, the actual danger of terrorist violence, and therefore its significance as a security issue, is widely misunderstood, in part because many states find the fear of terrorism to be politically useful. Before the GWOT and throughout its duration, the risk of dying in a terrorist attack was and has remained significantly lower than the chances of death by other violent means. In the United Kingdom, domestic violence killed fifteen times more people than terrorist attacks between 2000 and 2018. Similarly, between 1975 and 2016, US citizens had a greater chance of being killed in an animal attack than by terrorists. Of all deaths in 2017, 0.05 per cent were caused by terrorism.[34] Yet, in a series of opinion polls between 1995 and 2017, around 50 per cent of Americans reported that they were worried about being a victim of terrorist violence. Here again the media plays a part – coverage of terrorism (and violent forms of death, such as homicide, generally) receive far more media coverage than the actual frequency of such events would suggest.

The perceived threat of Islamist terrorism has also obscured the fact that most victims of terrorist violence are themselves Muslim, in large part because the greatest number of terrorist attacks take place in Muslim-majority countries. Other attacks, however, are explicitly targeted against Muslims. Aotearoa has experienced one such terrorist attack. On 15 March 2019, a terrorist killed fifty-one people at Al Noor Mosque and the Linwood Islamic Centre in Christchurch. The perpetrator had previously published his white supremacist views online in a so-called manifesto. The effects on Muslim communities in many Western nations is compounded, in that they remain disproportionately affected by state counter-terrorism measures due to the aforementioned misguided perception that Islamist terrorism is widespread.

The main point is that there are genuine reasons to question our reliance on military force as a means of security, and therefore good reasons to consider rethinking how we go about pursuing security. If military force is unreliable and unpredictable, unsuited to current violent threats like terrorism, and results in high levels of civilian casualties and social harm, then perhaps we need to reconsider its role in the maintenance of security.

Non-Military Threats and Dangers

As we noted in Chapter 1, and as the NZDF and Ministry of Defence themselves recognise in their reports and assessments, the greatest threats facing Aotearoa New Zealand are in fact not conventional military threats, but rather non-traditional threats like climate change, pandemics, cyber-crime, disinformation, terrorism and the like. Some non-miliary threats and dangers, such as the harms posed by the spread of lethal diseases like Covid-19, are obvious. In this case, the military has a limited role in securing and protecting people (notwithstanding the role of the NZDF in guarding quarantine hotels at the height of the crisis). The pandemic revealed that health security and other forms of security which stem from this, such as the free-flowing of global supply chains, are best achieved through having an appropriately trained and resourced health system, mechanisms for international cooperation and the willingness of political leaders to follow evidence-based public health advice.

Similarly, combat-trained military forces have a limited role to play in countering the effects of disinformation and conspiracy theories, and the political and social polarisation they engender. In fact, the deployment of force in such social conflicts can increase the potential for violence, thereby undermining people's sense of security. Such a threat requires a non-military approach focused on enhancing social cohesion and inclusion, expanded forms of dialogue, media regulation and the like. And we have already touched upon the failure of military force in dealing with the threat of terrorism and violent extremism. There is growing evidence that non-coercive approaches, such as preventing violent extremism programmes, dialogue-based initiatives, social reform and social cohesion measures, are more effective in reducing the threat of terrorism and political violence.[35]

In fact, the greatest security threat facing Aotearoa – and humankind itself – and the threat that is arguably the least amenable to a military solution, is the threat posed by the accelerating climate crisis. According to a special report by the Intergovernmental Panel on Climate Change (IPCC) in 2018, if the global temperature were to rise by 1.5 degrees Celsius, humans will face unprecedented climate-related risks and weather events. In actuality, we are on track for a temperature rise of 3–4 degrees, and even if the world cuts all emissions today, we are still set for rises due to the cumulative effect of carbon build-up on the climate.[36] The IPCC report recommends investing a great deal of money in climate mitigation measures, specifically about 2.5 per cent of global gross domestic product for two decades. But there is currently no evidence that any states anywhere are investing in such measures at this kind of level, even while many states, including Aotearoa, continue to expand their military spending.

Many of the impacts of climate change are already starting to manifest. They include rising sea levels and coastal flooding threatening hundreds of millions of people (whole Pacific islands, as well as many coastal regions, will soon become uninhabitable); an increase in extreme and destructive weather events which threaten lives and livelihoods, such as hurricanes, flooding and heat waves; costly and growing health impacts caused by the spread of viruses, bacteria, insect-borne diseases and the like; the destruction of marine ecosystems, including coral reefs, due to sea temperature rise; extinction events for many species and decreased biodiversity (according to a recent report, a million species are under threat);[37] pressures on ground water from droughts and/or increased precipitation; consequent disruptions to food supplies due to droughts, crop diseases and changing weather patterns; and more besides.

These and other effects mean that climate change is already having devastating effects on societies through death, injury, displacement and insecurity. The floods and tropical storm which led to unprecedented damage and some loss of life in Aotearoa in early 2023 is an example. The United Nations High Commissioner for Refugees, the UN's refugee agency, estimates that since 2008, more than 20 million people have been forcibly displaced from their homes by weather-related events such as floods, storms, fires and extreme temperatures. Referred to by some as 'climate change refugees' – people forced to migrate from their homes because climate change has undermined food production systems and livelihoods – and by others as 'climate migrants', their number is likely to increase over the coming decades, especially when rising sea levels make a great many cities uninhabitable, and food production systems are disrupted. A 2012 report by the humanitarian organisation DARA, commissioned by twenty different governments, estimates that about 5 million people die each year from air pollution, hunger and disease as a result of climate change and carbon-intensive economies.[38] That annual toll will likely rise to claim an estimated 100 million lives by 2030 if current patterns of fossil fuel use continue. More than 90 per cent of these deaths will occur in developing countries.

Given these trends and effects, researchers have been examining the link between climate change and conflict, including wars. The consensus of all the major studies of the past few years is that climate change is a significant, if indirect, cause of conflict.[39] It is what analysts call a 'threat multiplier' or 'conflict multiplier'. In other words, it is not that climate change directly or inevitably results in increased conflict; it depends in part on how societies respond to the issue. It can lead to increased competition and conflict or to greater cooperation. Nevertheless, there are a number of pathways by which the climate crisis is leading to increased conflict, violence and insecurity.

The mass displacement of people as a direct consequence of the climate crisis is one of the key ways the effects of climate change can indirectly lead to increased levels of conflict. Natural disasters are already believed to displace three times as many people as war and conflict. As more frequent natural disasters by way of storms, droughts, heat waves and extreme weather events occur, the number of people displaced by climate change effects is set to rise dramatically. More specifically, the World Bank Group has reported that the impacts of climate change in sub-Saharan Africa, South Asia and Latin America could result in the displacement and internal migration of more than 140 million people before 2050.[40] The IPCC says that regions in Africa within 15 degrees of the equator will suffer significantly from the global rise in temperatures, in the form of extended droughts, heat waves and crop failures, and with the Western Sahel region experiencing the strongest drying due to temperature rise. Because countries in these regions already have limited capacity to adapt, it's likely that economic conditions will deteriorate, violent conflicts over scarce resources like water will increase, and people will go on the move.

In a global sense, the climate crisis will undoubtedly lead to what we might call 'climate apartheid' – the intensification of inequality between the poorer countries of the world, many of whom are in regions where the negative effects of climate change will be most strongly experienced, and rich countries where climate change could actually help them to even greater levels of wealth and success. This will in turn create ever greater pressures on people to migrate to those wealthier, more stable regions. It has been estimated that the number of migrants arriving in the European Union could triple by the end of the century, and numbers seeking refuge in other countries and areas increase similarly. While the mass migration of people doesn't inevitably lead to conflict (it could also lead to a spirit of hospitality and welcome instead), it may well trigger increased inter-group violence, especially when societies don't have the capacity to absorb so many people, when they move into situations of already scarce resources and when identity politics – nationalism and xenophobia – are consequently stoked by politicians, certain sections of the media and extremist groups.

Another reason the climate crisis could lead to increased conflict, violence and insecurity is because it is already generating greater competition over scarce resources, including water itself, in regions that already struggle in this regard such as the Middle East and North Africa. Other crucial resources which could become scarce in certain regions include arable or grazing land, plants and crops, fish stocks and so on. In all societies, land is a source of daily material sustenance, and in many it is also a source of individual and group identity – many Indigenous and other communities around the world derive a spiritual or psychological identity through connection to the land. The problem is that when land becomes unusable or inaccessible through climate effects (such as erosion, flooding, salinisation, etc.), it can lead to increased competition, loss of identity, dislocation, and so on. Such emerging conflicts are already manifesting in some Pacific islands.

As already noted, this does not mean conflict is unavoidable. But there is certainly an enhanced risk that resource scarcity will generate intense competition between groups, elites, states and corporations – which in turn could lead to more violent conflict, especially in light of the global arms trade and in combination with rising nationalism. In other words, there is a strong likelihood that climate change will result in greater numbers of both internal civil wars and interstate wars.

A third indirect pathway from the climate crisis to conflict and insecurity is via the effects of economic crises and the failure of institutions to adapt. In both the global south and the global north, the costs associated with climate change directly (in terms of natural disasters, for example) and indirectly (in terms of adapting – relocating people from coastlines, for example) are going to be considerable. In both poor and rich countries, the resources needed will far outstrip what governments currently have or bring in by taxation, and in most countries, public institutions do not have the capacity to deal with the need. In other words, the economic costs of climate change and adaptation could lead to crises, increased poverty and increased inequality (as the wealthy are much more able to adapt and cope). We know from many studies that economic crises and state failures to assist people in need are often a trigger for corruption, exploitation by elites, public anger and, eventually, armed conflict and political violence.[41]

A final pathway from the climate crisis to insecurity is simply the levels of stress that climate change can create or exacerbate within communities and what might result from that stress. In communities that are already experiencing conflict over other issues, such as inequality or lack of recognition, adding the stresses of climate change can intensify the existing conflicts.

The broader issue is that through these different pathways, and notwithstanding that climate change is an indirect cause, we can predict with a fairly high degree of confidence that we are facing a world where levels of political and social conflict will intensify at the same time that the climate emergency does. As levels of general conflict increase, the likelihood of political violence will also increase. Along with the other obvious reasons, this is yet another example of why we need to consider climate change *the* most important security challenge of our generation and find effective ways to try to mitigate its harmful effects.

We can draw further conclusions by looking at the role of the military in the climate crisis. Not only is the combat-focused NZDF incapable of providing security from the climate change threat or dealing with the different pathways by which insecurity is generated, but the military as an institution is a major contributor to climate warming. A growing body of research demonstrates that the world's military forces are a huge contributor to greenhouse gas emissions – more than many major industrialised countries.[42] This is due to the fuel they use in transport, the manufacture and importation of weapons and equipment, their energy consumption, the fires they cause, the damage to environments from live-fire exercises, and so on. The problem is magnified by the fact that most nations withhold information on military emissions data and exclude the military from climate reduction agreements, so awareness of the issue is low and few militaries have faced pressure to reduce their emissions. Even fewer have made significant efforts to become carbon neutral. In the Pacific, scholars and activists have argued that the biennial Rim of the Pacific Exercise, in which the NZDF participates, causes environmental damage and contributes to the dispossession of Indigenous land in Hawai'i.[43] In short, given the nature and activities of the military, it is hard to see how they could ever become carbon neutral or make a positive contribution to climate change mitigation. In other words, the military, by its continuing existence as a major greenhouse gas emitter, is directly contributing to the growing insecurity caused by the climate crisis. It is a cause of climate crisis-induced insecurity, not a solution to it.

Summary

In this chapter, we have explored the dominant but conventional approach to national security used by Aotearoa New Zealand and its allies. Within the assumptions and perceptions of this approach, the main security threats facing a nation come from other states who might invade or engage in a military confrontation, and the primary means of security comes from a conventionally trained and equipped military. As we have demonstrated, however, this is a myth – a simple and comforting story about how to make a state secure. The reality in the twenty-first century is much more complex. The nature of military conflict itself has changed, as have the main threats facing the world and its people, and neither warfare nor non-conventional security threats like climate change are really amenable to resolution or management by military force. In fact, in this context, military force is all but redundant and may even be a contributor to insecurity. A sober and realistic assessment suggests that the military is an expensive anachronism that provides very little – if any – real security. On this assessment, there are grounds for seriously considering abolishing the NZDF and exploring whether other kinds of institutions and approaches might provide more relevant and lasting forms of security.

3. The Myth of the 'Good International Citizen'

One of the main arguments proffered for maintaining the New Zealand Defence Force is that a well-resourced military is necessary for meeting Aotearoa New Zealand's international obligations. In order to be a 'good international citizen' who contributes to the maintenance of a stable and peaceful international system, Aotearoa needs to be able to contribute to peacekeeping operations, humanitarian interventions, collective security and other international emergencies. In many ways, this is an appeal to Aotearoa's record of engagement in international affairs and the story we tell ourselves about the good we have done around the world in the past century or so.

However, a closer examination, we contend, once again reveals that this is more of a myth than an accurate reflection of reality. In fact, the record of the NZDF in peacekeeping and various wars reveals a very mixed set of outcomes, few of which have been unequivocally positive. On the whole, NZDF deployments, with only rare exceptions, have resulted in very little security benefit for the nations involved, nor have they contributed to making Aotearoa or the wider international system safer and more secure. In fact, it could be argued that Aotearoa's real contribution as a good international citizen comes from its nuclear disarmament leadership, its ethical foreign policy stands and its peacemaking efforts. These actions have contributed to making the world more peaceful and secure, and none of them involved deploying the NZDF.

The New Zealand Defence Force and International Peacekeeping

The NZDF has a long and, some would contend, illustrious history of being involved in United Nations peacekeeping operations. In 2011, Aotearoa New Zealand had 458 NZDF personnel participating in nineteen UN-led or UN-endorsed operations; in 2017, there were 219 personnel across fourteen operations in ten countries.[1] The decrease was noted by journalists Nicky Hager and Jon Stephenson, who argue that the NZDF is gradually being diverted away from peacekeeping missions towards more combat operations.[2] In any event, Aotearoa New Zealand's ability to continue to participate in such international efforts is another commonly cited argument for why we should maintain a military force.

The Aotearoa New Zealand government often uses the phrase 'peace support operations' to describe United Nations peacekeeping operations.[3] However, it is important to recognise that the term 'peace support operations' is also used in a way that includes peace enforcement operations (UN-sanctioned missions that are granted the power to use lethal military force to end hostilities, rather than solely in self-defence) and 'other military deployments based on alliance and other ties'.[4] What, then, have Aotearoa New Zealand's peace support operations involved? Over the past seventy years, the missions have included a wide variety of activities from unarmed observation and monitoring of ceasefires between armed groups (such as India and Pakistan), through to the type of work that was conducted in Afghanistan in which units of the New Zealand Special Air Service, Aotearoa New Zealand's special forces group, were deployed to conduct military operations.

Aotearoa New Zealand's operations have evolved alongside ever-changing notions of what constitutes peacekeeping, and related changes in the composition of international forces. Early UN missions typically had a more restricted mandate, and this is reflected in Aotearoa New Zealand's work during the 1950s in ceasefire monitoring operations in Kashmir and Sinai. Following the Cold War, these missions changed 'from a traditional, primarily military model of observing ceasefires and forces separations after inter-state wars, to a complex model of many elements, military and civilian, working together to build peace in the dangerous aftermath of civil wars'.[5] Peacekeeping and, beginning in the 1990s, peacebuilding operations became far more extensive and complex during this time – a time that saw Aotearoa make some of its largest contributions to international forces in places like Bougainville and Timor-Leste.

After 2001, a transition began whereby the proportion of NZDF personnel on UN deployments decreased relative to the proportion of personnel on non-UN deployments, such as those in Afghanistan and Iraq (from 2015).[6] Between 2002 and 2012, the number of troops deployed on UN missions never exceeded fifty. Over this same period, non-UN deployments increased, peaking at just over 500 in 2010.[7] While UN missions are not the only form of international peacekeeping, with some being led by regional organisations, the size of the contribution to such operations casts doubt on the widely held assumption that traditional peacekeeping operations are a large part of what the NZDF does. The government itself has admitted to reluctance to participate in UN peacekeeping operations due to the risk to personnel involved.[8]

In evaluating whether Aotearoa New Zealand should maintain a military in order to continue to participate in these types of operations, it would seem important to consider a number of key questions. First, how large a portion of the NZDF's work do these operations constitute? Second, what is the track record of success of these operations? And third, could the stated aims of these operations be achieved through alternative, nonviolent methods? In other words, is the NZDF in its current form really necessary for making this kind of contribution to the international community?

First, the evidence suggests that in recent years support for UN peace support missions has not been a major part of what the NZDF has done. In 2011, Aotearoa New Zealand contributed $22.2 million dollars to United Nations peacekeeping operations.[9] In the same year, the NZDF received around $2.77 billion from Aotearoa New Zealand's government budget. Clearly, the former is a much smaller figure than the latter.

Further, while some of the operations, such as those conducted in Timor-Leste and the Solomon Islands, had many positive achievements, there needs to be an objective assessment of the broader track record of UN peacekeeping and peacebuilding operations, as well as the particular peace support operations of which Aotearoa has been a part of. Making such an assessment will help us understand what has been achieved by past missions, but also whether we should continue to make similar contributions in future. Some of the failures of peace support operations, such as the disastrous failure in Afghanistan, have already been touched upon earlier.

In fact, the longer historical record of UN peacekeeping and peacebuilding is chequered at best and shameful at worst. There is a large body of research detailing failed UN interventions in Somalia, Rwanda, Bosnia, the Democratic Republic of Congo, Iraq, Afghanistan and others. In some of these cases, such as Rwanda and Bosnia, the failure of the UN directly resulted in genocide. UN peacekeepers have sometimes been responsible for war crimes, rape and sex trafficking. In other cases, UN operations have been relatively successful at stopping immediate violence and delivering disaster relief, but proved ineffective at the longer-term work of repairing and healing societies, establishing law and order, prosecuting war crimes and preventing future violence and insecurity. In large part, this is because the UN is subject to the interests of the great powers who dominate the Security Council, it employs a top-down, one-size-fits-all peace operation template to different countries and contexts, it focuses on elites and institutions and it imposes neoliberal economic and political policies on vulnerable societies.[10]

New Zealand has contributed to all major UN peace and stability operations in the Pacific, namely, in Bougainville, East Timor/Timor-Leste and Solomon Islands. In East Timor, in response to violence stemming from a referendum in 1999 in which the majority of the people of East Timor voted for independence from Indonesia, 1,100 NZDF personnel participated in the International Force East Timor (INTERFET), a non-UN peacekeeping mission led by Australia.[11] More than 5,000 NZDF personnel were deployed to East Timor between 1999 and 2002. Additional deployments took place as part of the UN-led International Stabilisation Force following a resurgence in violence in 2006. Up to 180 personnel were deployed at any one time during this latter part of the NZDF's work in Timor-Leste, which concluded in 2012. In total, over 7,400 NZDF personnel were deployed to Timor-Leste. The initial phase of the deployment to Timor-Leste was the NZDF's largest since the Korean War. Five personnel died, including the first combat fatality since the Vietnam War.

The deployment to Timor-Leste represents the high-water mark in terms of Aotearoa's contribution of personnel to UN peacekeeping (although many were deployed under the aegis of INTERFET, a non-UN mission). However, given the long-term and continuing poverty, instability and insecurity on the island, the operation, as with many other UN interventions, represents a marginal or at least rather modest success.

Similarly, the NZDF's deployment to Solomon Islands was prompted by civil conflict.[12] Between 1998 and 2003, more than a hundred people were killed and

40,000 displaced from their homes as armed factions clashed over control of land and political influence. The Townsville Peace Agreement (reached in late 2000) established the unarmed, Australian-led International Peace Monitoring Team (IPMT), intended to monitor the peace and specifically arms handed over by the fighting factions. Several of the IPMT staff were NZDF personnel, including the deputy commander. Despite the presence of the IPMT, the situation worsened. In response, the Regional Assistance Mission to Solomon Islands (RAMSI), also to be Australian-led, deployed to Solomon Islands to restore order:

> The RAMSI mission was under the auspices of the Pacific Island Forum and was largely funded and directed by Australia. Most of the 2200 military and police officers were from Australia and New Zealand and there was also personnel from other Pacific countries such as Fiji, Sāmoa and Tonga.[13]

In October 2003, there were 230 NZDF personnel working within RAMSI. Deployments (seventeen in total) continued until 2013, diminishing in size over time as the security situation improved. However, and once again, given the continuing violence and instability in the islands in 2023, it would be quite inaccurate to suggest that this represents a fully successful peace support operation, as some argue.

Of course, none of this is to suggest that these continuing historical failures are attributable to the work of Aotearoa New Zealand's peacekeepers or any individual peacekeepers. The point is simply that as these operations have such varied and often negative results, contributing to such operations surely cannot serve as a strong argument for maintaining the NZDF. This is especially true when we consider alternative means of intervening in situations of conflict and unrest. The reality is that there are effective alternatives to the use of armed peacekeepers as a means of intervening in conflict situations.

For instance, alongside a growing body of evidence that suggests that strategies of nonviolent resistance can be effective in overthrowing authoritarian regimes, winning human rights and protecting vulnerable people, there is now growing evidence for nonviolent civilian peacekeeping. What has been termed 'unarmed civilian peacekeeping' (UCP) involves groups of trained civilian peacekeepers who go into a conflict situation and use nonviolent techniques and unarmed approaches to protect other civilians from violence and the threat of violence, as well as to support local efforts to build peace.[14] This practice has been tried around the globe for decades with either no or close to no deaths of the civilian peacekeepers, even when they are confronting armed actors like rebel groups and state militaries. UCPs have operated in many conflict zones, including Guatemala, El Salvador, Colombia, Sri Lanka, Nepal, Sudan, Indonesia and Georgia, among others.[15] These examples have demonstrated that with the right training and techniques, it is possible to successfully protect civilians in conflict zones without the need for armed soldiers.[16] We discuss nonviolent approaches to security and conflict management further in the next chapter.

Interestingly, and relevant here, the best-known case of NZDF peacekeeping is its work in Bougainville. Conflict between an armed movement of Bougainvilleans and the government of Papua New Guinea, which centred on the contested presence of a large Australian-owned copper mine in the region, was ongoing between 1988 and 1997. There had been fourteen failed previous attempts at a peace settlement. Multiple rounds of peace talks were held in Aotearoa, the 1997 Burnham Truce establishing a ceasefire to immediate hostilities and clearing the way for the Truce Monitoring Group (TMG). The TMG was led by New Zealand and consisted of unarmed military and civilian personnel from New Zealand, Australia, Fiji and Vanuatu whose mandates were to patrol and monitor the truce to ensure that it was observed. New Zealand provided 250 personnel from December 1997 until April 1998.

The NZDF's work in Bougainville is well known for several reasons. In the first instance, this peacekeeping work was the earliest of the major peacekeeping operations conducted by the NZDF in the Pacific. Moreover, the conflict itself was particularly violent and protracted. Fatalities are often estimated at 15,000 to 20,000 people, with conservative figures of between 1,000 to 2,000. In either case, it was the deadliest armed conflict in the Pacific since World War II. Finally, the approaches taken by New Zealand's peacekeepers were entirely nonviolent, relying on, among other things, artistic exchange in the form of song and dance, underpinned by a broader cultural exchange that emphasised Māoritanga and the role of women in peacekeeping work. Due to the success of the mission (Bougainville remains politically stable today) and its unusual features, notably the decision to send unarmed soldiers, the Bougainville deployment is a cornerstone of the popular notion that Aotearoa is a keen peacekeeping nation, and one that employs a 'Kiwi way' in peacekeeping operations.[17]

Yet despite the history of involvement in deployments in the Pacific, and even though the number of troops deployed to the Middle East has diminished in recent years, at present, and for the better part of the past two decades, the deployments of the NZDF show a pattern of collaboration with the US–Anglo alliance, largely in the Middle East and environs. Aotearoa's intervention in Bougainville occurred in the 1990s, and the largest component of the deployment to Timor-Leste concluded in 2002. Similarly, the height of the NZDF's contributions to RAMSI came in 2003. Since then, there has been no major NZDF engagement in the Pacific, the largest deployments being ad hoc responses to events such as natural disasters. These peacekeeping operations further demonstrate that much of the good achieved through this work is via nonviolent means, even in cases of extreme violent conflict such as Bougainville. This once again raises the question of whether a combat-ready, military force is a requirement of continuing to play a positive, impactful role in the Pacific and wider international community.

The New Zealand Defence Force and Anglosphere Wars

Alongside peacekeeping, the NZDF's most significant deployments have been in support of its major allies, often referred to as the Anglosphere. The Anglosphere describes a core group of countries which share historical and cultural ties with the United Kingdom, and consequently, have close political, diplomatic and military cooperation. The group includes the United Kingdom, the United States, Canada, Australia and New Zealand. The establishment of the settler colony in Aotearoa by the United Kingdom is the origin of the close ties between New Zealand and the Anglosphere, and it is significant that all the members of the group, apart from the United Kingdom, are settler-colonial states. It is also significant that, as we saw in Chapter 1, the precursor to the NZDF was employed to suppress Māori opposition to colonisation and to take Māori land, while the first foreign engagements of New Zealand's military forces were in support of the British Empire.

These close cultural and historical ties have led to Aotearoa's participation – some would say co-option or entanglement – in numerous wars over the past century or more. Following the New Zealand Wars that attempted to suppress Indigenous resistance and establish the New Zealand settler state, military forces from Aotearoa were sent to fight in the South African 'Boer' War, followed by World Wars I and II. Later, New Zealand forces joined the United States and United Kingdom in the conflicts in Korea, Malaya, Borneo, Vietnam and the first Gulf War. More recently,

New Zealand has fought with the Anglosphere in Afghanistan and Iraq in the US-led GWOT. It is highly questionable whether any of these wars could be assessed as having contributed to greater international peace and security, and some of them, most notably the Vietnam War, were a divisive and contentious failure, and revealed that Aotearoa was willing to sacrifice peace and security for allyship.

Some policymakers and pundits have argued that Aotearoa's staunch allyship with the Anglosphere is based on a genuine belief that United States and Anglosphere global leadership is the best way to maintain a stable liberal international order. However, from another perspective, there are ways in which the so-called liberal international order is both racist and subservient to Western self-interest, especially from the perspective of countries in large parts of the global south, and that this order has been a major source of injustice, conflict and instability, rather than peace and stability. The history of Western military intervention in regions like the Middle East and Latin America, for example, support for coups and dictators, political assassination and covert interference in other states during the Cold War, would seem to belie a real commitment to a liberal world order. The same conclusion can be reached when we consider the illegal invasion of Iraq in 2003 as part of the GWOT, and the fallout from the invasions of Afghanistan and Iraq when widespread torture, human rights abuses, the Guantanamo Bay prison camp and questionable drone killings were revealed.

Others argue that Aotearoa's close relations with the powerful Anglosphere states provides a security guarantee in case China or some other hostile power threatens our territory. However, this is also debatable given Aotearoa's withdrawal from the ANZUS Treaty in the 1980s, New Zealand's recent omission from the AUKUS security pact, and the minor strategic value of the country to the United States. It seems doubtful that the United States would risk a major confrontation that could escalate to nuclear war in defence of New Zealand. The assumption that they would come to our aid should not be employed as a basis for real-world political decisions. In fact, looking at it from another perspective, Aotearoa's close relations with the United States could be putting us at greater risk from such external threats – neutrality could be a more reliable security guarantee. In any case, as we demonstrated in Chapter 1, strategic assessments suggest that this is a very minor risk.

A great many policymakers and pundits argue that, as important as any security guarantee, there are concrete economic, diplomatic and security benefits to New Zealand's close alliance with the Anglosphere. The country benefits, they say, from our willing participation in Anglosphere wars and our close security cooperation in groups like the Five Eyes. However, this is also arguable and in need of a thorough public debate. It could be argued instead, for example, that particularly since Aotearoa's nuclear-free declaration, the nation's economic success has come not from preferential treatment as a reward for allyship, but through pivoting towards the Asia-Pacific and pursuing free trade agreements. Similarly, it could be argued that such close allyship with the Anglosphere, particularly in the GWOT, has actually negatively affected the nation, because we are seen as supporters of US actions and hegemony.

At base, there is a real tension between Aotearoa's desire to contribute to a rules-based, peaceful international system, its deep commitment to anti-nuclearism and disarmament, its desire to conduct an ethical foreign policy and its historic loyalty to the Anglosphere. On a number of occasions, and in a number of ways (such as its continued participation in the Five Eyes intelligence system), the New Zealand government has chosen to support the Anglosphere with military contributions that have lacked popular support and international legitimacy, and which have arguably contributed to international instability and conflict, rather than peace and stability. The Vietnam War stands out as an example of this during the Cold War period, while the Afghanistan war is a more recent example from the GWOT.

The Afghanistan deployment in support of the US-led coalition was the longest foreign war in Aotearoa's history.[18] Despite being characterised as a humanitarian intervention, Aotearoa's participation was primarily political and military, as it moved in solidarity with the United States.[19] For example, it emerged that one of the key roles of the New Zealand Special Air Service (SAS) units operating in Afghanistan was to paint targets for US bombs. Investigations by Nicky Hager and Jon Stephenson demonstrated that the humanitarian-aid-related roles of the NZDF were at best minimal, ineffective and unsustainable. More damagingly, they brought allegations of war crimes committed by the NZDF in retaliation attacks.[20] Overall, as we discussed in the previous chapter, the occupation of Afghanistan as part of the GWOT was a strategic, political and humanitarian disaster which likely cost over a million lives, destabilised the broader Middle East region and increased the number of terrorist attacks and terrorist groups operating around the world. As such, it demonstrated the clear limits of military force for creating security, democracy and development, and put paid to Aotearoa's claims to being a 'good global citizen'.

Crucially, it can be shown that there have been gradual institutional changes within the NZDF itself which reflect and have contributed to Aotearoa's orientation towards the Anglosphere. Specifically, the growing influence of the SAS within the NZDF has coincided with the general reduction in peacekeeping training and deployments, and an increase in SAS deployments in Anglosphere military operations. Hager and Stephenson's research suggests that the SAS has pushed for more involvement in Anglosphere military operations at the expense of peacekeeping missions.[21] This reorientation of the role of the NZDF has occurred without any major public debate.

In sum, we do not believe that we need the NZDF for assisting our Anglosphere allies, especially given the past twenty years of the war on terror which has directly led to increased and widespread violence, instability and insecurity around the world. Aotearoa's military support of the Anglosphere has failed to provide genuine benefits in terms of trade preference, security guarantees and protection. In fact, given the role of the Anglosphere in generating international instability and insecurity, particularly its illegal and at times immoral interventions in the Middle East and Afghanistan, it could be reasonably argued that Aotearoa's greatest contribution to international peace and security would be to withdraw from cooperation with the Anglosphere and devote itself instead to diplomatic peacemaking, disarmament and neutrality. As we have already noted, Aotearoa's cultural traditions and historical ties are more diverse than is commonly acknowledged. Our peace traditions and leadership in nuclear disarmament, for example, could provide the basis for a new, more peaceful, more ethical foreign policy orientation. This proposition ought to be up for serious public discussion.

Summary

It is common for politicians and pundits to point to Aotearoa's historic involvement in peacekeeping operations and military conflicts on the side of our Anglosphere allies as compelling reasons for why the NZDF is an essential tool of foreign policy. As we have demonstrated in this chapter, this claim is based on a rather rosy view of a much more complicated and unsettling record. It is, in other words, another myth – a comforting story we tell ourselves about why we keep sending soldiers off to risk their lives in foreign wars even when the outcomes are, in reality, ambiguous. In some ways, it is a useful myth for the political and military elites to justify the continued expense involved in maintaining the NZDF. Would the public really support the sacrifice in lives and treasure if it knew that such operations were not genuinely necessary to being a good international citizen but instead were designed primarily to maintain favour with powerful nations and were in fact largely ineffective?

In this chapter, we have tried to illustrate both that the deployment of military force in pursuit of being a 'good international citizen' has not been as successful as is commonly believed and that, in fact, there could be alternatives. Instead of deploying the NZDF to fight with its allies or participate in UN peace support operations, Aotearoa could instead develop and support unarmed civilian peacekeepers, use its good diplomatic offices to try to resolve international conflicts, and pursue good international citizenship by continuing its leadership in nuclear disarmament. In fact, Aotearoa could embrace its longstanding and culturally rooted peace traditions and lead the way in general disarmament, thereby making a genuine contribution to international peace and security and proving its worth as a good international citizen.

4. The Myth of No Alternatives to Military Force

There is no question that international terrorism, authoritarian regimes and armed violence in general cause a great deal of human suffering and international instability. Solutions are required and Aotearoa should be an active participant in devising those solutions. In highlighting the limits and failures of military violence across multiple areas, we are not suggesting that Aotearoa should turn its back on these challenges, nor are we suggesting that there are obvious or easy solutions to be had. We simply contend that there are a number of key reasons, including the tragic failures of the twenty-plus years of the global war on terror, which demand a rethink of Aotearoa's options for responding to international security challenges. In particular, we argue that there are options that do not require us to maintain an expensive military force. The potential for non-military means of responding to international security challenges such as terrorism and authoritarianism are very promising, even if they are currently under-researched and under-resourced. Many of these options remain in an embryotic stage of their development, requiring serious investment and effort to realise their full potential.

What we are suggesting is that nonviolent alternatives to the military do exist. Some are based on the organised action of civilians, as is the case with nonviolent peoples' movements that have challenged and overthrown many oppressive regimes around the world. This is also true of civilian-based actions to deter and resist invasion attempts from foreign states, or to protect communities in the midst of civil wars. Other alternatives are not based on civilian action and would require the creation of new nonviolent institutions with specific skillsets and resources aimed at tackling tasks that New Zealand Defence Force personnel may currently be called on to conduct. These include peacekeeping and civilian protection in conflict zones, relief and rescue work after disasters, the security of the environment and fisheries, cyber-security and even national defence. Arguably, nonviolent approaches could be more effective in these areas, where the training and equipment of a military force that is primarily prepared for war-fighting is not. Additionally, and very importantly, there are social, environmental, political, security and financial benefits which could flow from employing these means as compared to the current military means.

Challenging Authoritarian Regimes

We have already discussed the limits and failures of military force, including the NZDF's record in peacekeeping and military assistance to its Anglosphere allies. It is often argued that military intervention by states like Aotearoa is necessary to overthrow authoritarian rulers; this was certainly one of the arguments for the NZDF's deployment to Afghanistan. Western democratic states, such as New Zealand, have long used the presence of a dictator or an authoritarian regime in a foreign country as a justification for the invasion and sometimes occupation of those countries. Alternatively, if they do not invade, states may offer military support and weaponry to armies within a foreign country that will attack a dictator or authoritarian regime from within. Shortly, we will outline nonviolent approaches to challenging and overthrowing such regimes, but, before we do, it is important to point out that there are good reasons to be sceptical of arguments by states who want to militarily intervene in other states, even when they claim that it is in pursuit of peace, security, democracy, human rights and the like.

In the first place, and for the most part, states act in their own self-interest, often engaging in actions overseas primarily in pursuit of material or political gain. In this context, arguments about improving the lives of others through military intervention and occupation can be used by governments to gain the support of their own populations and justify violent interventions which are in reality for self-interest. This approach was openly used by the colonial powers, including the colonisation of Aotearoa itself, and has continued to be used by powerful states to the present day. Russia's invasion of Ukraine in early 2022, for example, was justified to the Russian people on the grounds that it was necessary to protect Russian minorities from genocide by Ukrainian fascists. The fact is that military intervention in other nations is rarely advocated when there is no clear gain for the intervening country.

In addition, states, even Western states who express a commitment to human rights and democracy, have been quite happy to back and support authoritarian regimes when it fits with their interests, and even assist in the overthrow of democratic governments if they present a challenge to the intervening state's goals. The United States and United Kingdom, for example, supported numerous authoritarian regimes in Africa, Asia and Latin America during the Cold War. In the more recent GWOT, the West has supported deeply oppressive and corrupt regimes in places like Uzbekistan, Pakistan and Afghanistan because they were seen as partners in the fight against terrorism. The United States and United Kingdom have also participated in attempts to overthrow numerous democratically elected governments around the world, most recently in Venezuela.

Second, states are normally very selective about when they will risk their military forces to intervene in another nation, most often doing so only when it fits with a series of other interests or objectives. While a justification for maintaining a military might be to intervene in situations of extreme violence and human rights abuses, in practice, as we've seen over the past few decades, Western states have failed to respond even in the most egregious situations, such as in the genocides in Cambodia, Uganda, Rwanda, Bosnia and Darfur, along with Syria where chemical weapons were used against civilians, and Myanmar where Rohingya Muslims were being massacred.

Third, even when states do militarily intervene to try to protect civilians or establish democracy, the intervention often has negative or unforeseen outcomes. For example, there have been cases where humanitarian intervention has resulted in bolstering the position of an authoritarian ruler. When NATO attacked the Federal Republic of Yugoslavia in 1999, for example, the intervention inadvertently increased support for Slobodan Milošević from within the Serbian population. This was due in large part to the civilian casualties which resulted from the bombings, and the widespread destruction of infrastructure, and it gave Milošević the opportunity to paint himself as the protector of the country against foreign attack. Interestingly, Milošević was eventually overthrown and sent to the Hague to face a war crimes tribunal not by military intervention but by a nonviolent peoples' movement, which in turn sparked further nonviolent revolutions against other dictators in the region.

These three reasons alone could support the argument against maintaining a military for intervention overseas. Crucially, this does not mean that authoritarian rulers cannot be challenged and removed, leaving space for more democratic, freer and less violent societies. An alternative to external military intervention might be to support an army to fight against a regime within their own country. For example, the NZDF could provide weaponry and other equipment, such as training and logistical support, without directly engaging in a conflict themselves. In fact, the NZDF was sent to Europe in early 2022 to do exactly this for the Ukrainian military in their efforts against the Russian invasion.[1]

However, supporting other military forces does little to alleviate the wider concerns we have raised about military intervention. The consequences of war are the same. This type of action can, again, rarely be separated from the supporting state's own interests, and can also result in negative unforeseen consequences. We saw this many times during the Cold War, as either the Soviet Union or the United States backed one side of a conflict without directly engaging with each other's military – what was called 'proxy war'. In many cases, including Angola, Mozambique, Ethiopia, Nicaragua and elsewhere, such external military support for the different factions prolonged the fighting for many years and led to millions of casualties and refugees, and widespread devastation. Regardless, whatever the motivation for backing an armed group, it has become increasingly clear that military intervention has a poor track record when it comes to building free, secure and democratic post-conflict, post-authoritarian societies. In fact, it has a poor record of success in general, but a consistent record of causing a great many civilian casualties and societal destruction.

So, what are the nonviolent options in such situations? A growing and robust body of evidence suggests that nonviolent peoples' movements may be the most effective way that authoritarian regimes are removed from power, from within a society.[2] This research shows that nonviolent movements have been far more successful than violent resistance movements at overthrowing authoritarian regimes, providing a significant challenge to the idea that violence or military force is necessary to do so.

A groundbreaking and widely cited study by political scientists Erica Chenoweth and Maria J. Stephan in

2011 found that between 1900 and 2006, nonviolent campaigns achieved their goals of overthrowing a government, or of secession from a government, almost twice as often as violent campaigns. Violent movements within a country succeeded in overthrowing a regime 26 per cent of the time, whereas nonviolent campaigns were successful 53 per cent of the time.[3] On top of this, movements that used a combination of violent and nonviolent methods were also more likely to succeed than violent movements, but less likely to succeed than nonviolent movements.[4] This suggests that using a diversity of violent and nonviolent tactics and approaches to challenging dictatorship can sometimes undermine the success of nonviolent action.

In addition, nonviolent movements create much more preferable long-term outcomes than violent movements. There is less chance of civil war or large-scale violence following a nonviolent revolution when compared to violent revolutions, and there are increased levels of democracy which last longer.[5] Many of these outcomes occur even when the nonviolent revolutions fail, as compared to successful violent revolutions which tend to result in further violence in subsequent years.[6]

There are good explanations for the better long-term outcomes which follow a successful nonviolent revolution. For example, nonviolent movements tend to be more democratic in their organising and are less likely to centralise power after they take control; they are more inclusive, involving a wider demographic of people from across society in action; and they create power by imposing reversible costs, unlike violent movements which cause irreversible death and suffering.[7] This last point is particularly significant, because it highlights the condition that a post-conflict society is in after a political transition. Violent conflict, in addition to the deaths and injuries it causes to people, most often destroys vital infrastructure such as hospitals, roads, houses and schools, and undermines economic, political and cultural life. This leaves society in a fragile, vulnerable state in which further conflict and insecurity is more likely.

The psychological consequences of war and violence are also avoided or greatly reduced when nonviolent action is the primary mode of struggle. Generally, nonviolent action does not have the same psychological consequences for civilians: in war, civilian victims and survivors are more likely to experience violence, pain and the death of others. These are the inevitable consequences of the use of organised violence, and they can lead to widespread trauma, grievances and intergroup tensions. Nonviolent actions do not have the same consequences because they don't intentionally cause physical injury to human beings. While violence can still be a response to nonviolent action, violence occurs much less often and is much less destructive of infrastructure.

In addition, nonviolence does not have to impose the moral and psychological injury on military personnel that training for the military does. Just like civilian victims and survivors, those who fight in war also experience violence, pain and the death of others. They have to deal with the psychological consequences of both killing people and training to kill people.[8] This is sometimes called 'moral injury', in part because it involves breaking down the internal psychological barriers to killing and hurting others that humans are socialised into from birth. Soldiers have to disfigure their own sense of empathy for fellow human beings, for example, in order to effectively fight. The experience of being trained to kill, of killing in war and of witnessing killing in war often leads to post-traumatic stress disorder (PTSD), high rates of suicide and other psychological problems for soldiers when they try to return to civilian life.[9]

Interestingly, while nations often debate the financial cost of the military, they rarely debate the human costs in terms of PTSD, suicide, homelessness and the like which inevitably occur among former military personnel. We would argue that the psychological costs of the military, both in terms of the harms done to soldiers and the costs to society of caring for morally injured soldiers, ought to be part of the government's calculations and public debate about the costs of the NZDF. In Aotearoa, the military disproportionately recruits from among Māori and Pacific populations, such as the Services Academies programme for secondary schools which directs students towards a career in the NZDF.[10] Consequently, this means that these communities suffer disproportionately from any PTSD, inter-generational violence, homelessness and the like resulting from military service.

In many respects, the research on nonviolence raises important questions about whether the NZDF should take any offensive military actions in other countries, and whether Aotearoa should ever support military action overseas – not to mention the millions of dollars spent on efforts to recruit young people straight from school. The evidence strongly suggests that overseas military intervention, or even the indirect support of military fighting, rarely leads to lasting peaceful outcomes. On the other hand, nonviolent peoples' movements show much more promise for overthrowing authoritarian regimes, protecting vulnerable populations and creating peaceful societies, and therefore contributing to greater international security. As we have made clear so far in this book, nonviolent movements do not require the kind of support that the NZDF can offer. Given these findings, it might be better to divert financial resources from the NZDF and invest them instead in research, training and support for nonviolent movements. The NZDF budget might also be better used to support efforts aimed at diplomacy, conflict resolution, reconciliation, disaster relief, human rights protection and economic reconstruction in conflict zones.

It is important to note that exactly how nonviolent movements can be successfully supported from the outside is still relatively unknown, and foreign support may not even be preferable in some cases. Nonviolent revolutions are very much driven by peoples' movements (the mechanisms of which we will describe shortly), but significantly, nonviolent movements can learn from others. For example, leaders of Otpor, a resistance group in the former Yugoslavia, read the work of nonviolence scholars, and after successfully overthrowing Milošević they also worked with activists in other countries. Importantly, the work was done by themselves. Foreign powers may be able to supply resources, but how much this would help a movement is questionable and is likely to vary a lot in different situations. It could run the risk of making a movement look inauthentic or under the influence of foreign powers.

What is clear, however, is that embracing nonviolence does not readily support the neocolonial ambitions of other countries. A policy shift to disband the NZDF could be viewed as a statement by the New Zealand government against neocolonial intervention, as it would be removing some of its ability to engage in the international community this way, and its ability to align with other states that act in this way. The SAS could not be used to support Anglosphere intervention in the Middle East if it didn't exist, for example.

How Nonviolence Creates Change

It's all very well to say that nonviolence is more effective than violence at ousting authoritarian rulers, but how does it actually work? Many have understood and utilised the power of nonviolence in the past, from Te Whiti-o-Rongomai and Tohu Kākahi at Parihaka, to Mahatma Gandhi in South Africa and India and Martin Luther King Jr in the United States. The importance of their actions and writings on the subject cannot be underestimated. However, here we are going to draw on the work of American political scientist Gene Sharp (1928–2018), the world's most famous scholar of nonviolent revolution, whose theories of nonviolent action were born from observing nonviolent movements throughout history. Sharp's theory of pragmatic nonviolence has been central to much of the recent academic scholarship concerning unarmed movements. His work is translated into many languages and has been used by a great many nonviolent revolutionary movements to plan and execute successful nonviolent action to oust dictators, win concessions from rulers and inaugurate democratic politics. This is especially true of one of his most popular books, *From Dictatorship to Democracy* (1993), which has been used as something of a manual for overthrowing governments without military action.[11]

Sharp noted that political regimes, no matter how powerful or oppressive, are held up by the support of key groups within the population. These groups perform tasks that give rulers their power. These can be described as the 'pillars of support' of a ruler, and without these supports a ruler cannot exert power and has no real control. The secret to nonviolent action therefore is that the power of any government – democratic or authoritarian – ultimately rests with ordinary people's willingness to be ruled. Even in the most brutal totalitarian dictatorship, individuals or groups other than the dictator need to perform certain roles for the dictator to possess any real power: the media must generate propaganda to promote the dictator's popularity or power; the military and police must carry out operations to suppress opposition and enforce state control; bureaucrats must perform their tasks in order to ensure the basic functionality of a government; workers, especially those in vital industries, must continue their jobs in order to avoid economic recession or collapse; and the people must obey government edicts.

Sharp contended that where civilians, working together, remove or co-opt enough 'pillars' supporting a regime, the regime was bound to collapse. Notably, Sharp believed that armed violence was not required to achieve this. In fact, nonviolent resistance was pragmatic, Sharp argued, because a government (particularly an oppressive one) typically possesses the preponderance of military means in a society. To confront a dictatorship militarily, therefore, is to confront a dictatorship on terms to which it is well suited and well prepared. The chances of winning such a confrontation are low and very costly.

Sharp went on to outline 198 methods of nonviolent action which civilians could use to remove (or at least extract concessions from) oppressive regimes.[12] These were split into three main categories: protest and persuasion; non-cooperation; and direct intervention. Many of Sharp's actions move from demanding change from a government to exerting coercive force to create change. The list of methods includes actions such as demonstrations and protests, sit-ins and occupations, establishing free media, disrupting essential services, workers' strikes, boycott of electoral processes, ostracisation of individuals supporting the regime, boycott of retailers supporting the regime, the creation of parallel social and political institutions, civil disobedience, and many more.

The aim of all such actions, Sharp suggested, should be to induce or coerce those supporting the regime to cease such support, and perhaps even transfer their support to the unarmed movement. Of course, the pillars that hold up a regime, and the ability of unarmed movements to remove any one of those pillars, vary greatly from context to context. Different pillars will be more important in different contexts. There is no one-size-fits-all approach for nonviolent movements, and Sharp's work puts a strong emphasis on the need for careful planning, experimentation and strategic adaptation to the counter-measures that the regime takes.

As recent research demonstrates, nonviolent action of the type Sharp described has been successful in numerous cases, including, for example, the People Power movement in 1986 which brought down the Marcos regime in the Philippines, the Carnation Revolution which ended the military dictatorship in Portugal in 1974, and the peaceful revolutions in Poland, Czechoslovakia, East Germany, Ukraine, Bulgaria, Romania, Mongolia and the Baltic republics which contributed to the collapse of the Iron Curtain and the end of the Cold War.[13] After the collapse of the Soviet Union, a series of nonviolent revolutions swept across Africa and other parts of the developing world during what was called the 'Third Wave of Democracy', which transformed the face of the global south. More recently, nonviolent movements have taken place across the Middle East and North Africa in the Arab Spring, and the so-called 'Colour Revolutions' across Eastern Europe. It can be argued that these nonviolent movements, even when they do not result in immediate lasting change, have contributed to a more peaceful and democratic international system in ways that wars and military interventions decidedly have not.

Nonviolent Social Defence Against the Threat of Invasion

As we have already discussed, even if Aotearoa decided never to deploy the NZDF overseas again, there is still a persistent myth that the NZDF is needed, alongside Anglosphere allies, to defend the nation against invading forces. As we have explained, the NZDF itself thinks that the possibility of invasion is extremely unlikely. We have also argued that even if another state did invade Aotearoa, it is very unlikely that the NZDF could effectively defend against such a force, despite the vast resources that are put into it. In order to reach New Zealand territory and occupy the country, an invading military force is likely to be much larger and more powerful than anything the NZDF could realistically repel. Although the New Zealand government spends a large amount of money per capita on maintaining the NZDF, the NZDF is still a small military force compared to the defence forces of many countries with larger populations.

If there were a major change to the international security environment and Aotearoa was at risk of invasion, nonviolent options for defence could conceivably be more successful than the military option, and because of this they could also be more of a deterrent. The government's commitment to maintaining the NZDF for defence has so far blinded it to exploring other nonviolent options that may be more suitable to defending a small state in the face of foreign invasion. Moreover, nonviolent options would not require the purchase and maintenance of expensive military technology and would, therefore, be significantly cheaper. Such an approach would also have other social benefits, such as reducing military carbon emissions, among others.

Perhaps the key nonviolent alternative to military defence is what has been called civilian-based defence (CBD) or 'social defence'. Gene Sharp defines civilian-based defence as 'national defense against internal usurpations and foreign invasions by prepared nonviolent noncooperation and defiance by the population and the societies' institutions'.[14] Civilian-based defence works using the same model of people power we described earlier. As with nonviolent resistance to an authoritarian regime, nonviolent methods of protest and persuasion, non-cooperation and direct intervention are used to undermine the invader's pillars of support. A successful occupation by an invading force is not achieved by capturing government buildings or strategic installations. Rather, it requires systematic control of the population and key infrastructure.

In other words, invading forces still need pillars of support to maintain their occupation and achieve their aims. CBD is a defence policy that recognises and prepares for this possibility. Nonviolent methods can be used to make it very difficult for an invading force to access these pillars in the first place, and if the country is occupied, these methods could make the country unrulable and the occupation prohibitively expensive. If civilian action is well planned, it could be a very difficult obstacle for an occupying force to overcome – likely much more difficult than a miliary operation to defeat the NZDF. In short, civilian-based defence could act as a greater deterrence because it can form a larger, more complex and more resilient defence system.

To give some practical examples, if a foreign power invaded, roads, airport runways and ports could be blocked by vehicles and ships, making it difficult for the initial invading forces. People could change road signs to confuse the invading forces, something that Czechoslovakians did following the Prague Spring in 1968 to resist the invasion of Soviet forces. However, these kinds of actions would likely impose costs and delays only to the invasion itself. Once the invading army had occupied the country, actions by CBD could include things like the holding of strikes that stop government ministries and agencies from doing their jobs, refusing to maintain the infrastructure and refusing to work on resource extraction. The police could refuse to arrest people on strike, and media workers and teachers could refuse to spread an invader's propaganda. Workers could sabotage and disrupt communications signals, electricity supplies and transportation networks, while collective acts of defiance could be used to show opposition to the regime and build morale. Civilians could communicate with the invading forces and build relationships to encourage them to disobey orders or defect. Power supplies could be decentralised, by installing solar and wind generators in each neighbourhood, for example, so that a central power supply couldn't be cut off by an occupying regime. The food supply could also be decentralised through food grown in community gardens and allotments, which would similarly make the population less vulnerable to coercive control.

All of these types of actions, if they were planned, coordinated and enacted in a widespread and disciplined way, would make it extremely difficult for the invasion force to gain or maintain control of the territory and population. The cumulative effect would be to make the invasion and occupation excessively costly, thereby forcing a recalculation of the expected gains. It would also undermine the pillars of support necessary to maintain a ruling government, and could eventually lead to the collapse of the occupying government. And, because it was nonviolent, it would turn world opinion particularly strongly against the invading nation, perhaps leading to international boycotts, sanctions and disinvestment.

Civilian-based defence is not a new idea. The Gandhian movement in India explored a similar idea after Gandhi's death. The Shanti Sena, or peace army, was a concept envisioned by Gandhi and organised by the Sarvodaya movement after the British left India.[15] It took the form of a group of civilians who would engage in a range of activities, including the nonviolent defence of villages, intervention in riots, and peacekeeping activities. Members of the Shanti Sena were trained experts in nonviolent methods positioned within the community. Later, in the early 1990s, Lithuanians, Latvians and Estonians used nonviolent civilian-based defence techniques to resist invasion and occupation by Soviet forces, which were at that time trying to prevent the break-up of the Soviet Union, and eventually win their full independence. The holding of huge demonstrations, surrounding Soviet tanks with thousands of people and mass civil disobedience eventually persuaded the Soviet forces to pull out.

CBD could be utilised in Russia's ongoing invasion and occupation of Ukraine – a topic that scholars had been discussing well before the invasion.[16] Today, nonviolent methods that were previously used against the Soviet Union by civilians in Czechoslovakia, Lithuania, Latvia and Estonia could be deployed to oppose the Russian military, and in some cases already have been. In the current invasion, Ukrainian citizens have been changing street signs to confuse or send messages to Russian soldiers, and blocking tanks and other vehicles – among many other examples.

Ukrainian citizens are familiar with nonviolent resistance. Two revolutions, the first in 2004 and the second in 2014, used nonviolent methods to overthrow the Ukrainian government. Knowledge gained during these revolutions could be used and shared so that citizens can plan, organise, mobilise, challenge and undermine the Russian military without weapons. It is true that resisting an invading force would demand different strategies and actions to resisting a sitting government. However, the Ukrainian experience in using nonviolent resistance could form a valuable basis for identifying and targeting the pillars of support of the invading force. Knowledge about what nonviolent tactics have worked to repel invading forces elsewhere could also be shared and learned from. In addition, in 2014, nonviolent visible actions of citizens, including protests and street patrols, made it difficult for pro-Russian separatists to claim they had the support of the populace.[17] Similar actions could be used today – and there are some indications they already are – to undermine Russian claims.

In addition to the nonviolent methods we have already mentioned in this book, nonviolent techniques can be used to encourage members of the invading force to disobey orders, or even mutiny. A mutiny of troops would remove the Russian state's ability to inflict violence and thus undermine its power. The maintenance of nonviolent discipline may be necessary to encourage mutinies, as troops may be less willing to attack people who are not a threat to them.[18] With this in mind, citizens could go further and actively reach out to Russian soldiers through conversations, broadcasts, pamphlets and signage. They could convey messages of connectedness and emphasise the similarities between themselves, aiming to problematise or break down the concepts of 'us and them', or the idea of an enemy. Alternatively, or additionally, they may communicate arguments as to why the invasion is unjust – a technique used in the Czech resistance to the Soviet Union in 1968.[19]

Ideally, a country that adopted CBD would do so before an invasion took place. This was not the case in Ukraine. However, Lithuania is an example of a country that has put civilian-based defence into its national defence plan in case it is threatened by an invading force in the future. This is, in part, because the Lithuanian government is aware that its military could not defend the country against an attack from Russia, and any attempt to do so would lead to mass casualties and the utter destruction of the country.[20] Based on its earlier success, and wider research and theories about CBD, in 2015 the Lithuanian

118

government issued booklets with information about civilian defence to its citizens.

Aotearoa's position in an invasion scenario is quite similar to Lithuania's, where successful military defence conducted by the NZDF is simply unrealistic and would most likely result in widespread death and destruction. Of course, a civilian-based defence plan for New Zealand would need to be based on systematic research and then civilian involvement, training and preparation. Crucially, there is a large and sophisticated theoretical and empirical literature on civilian national defence models that both outlines strategies for implementing CBD and reports on historical cases of its use.[21] This broader research could form the foundation for this reform of Aotearoa's defence strategy. Importantly, CBD is not seen as completely unrealistic or untenable by all political parties in New Zealand. The Green Party of New Zealand, for example, has the exploration of CBD as one of their policies.[22] Having said this, there is still a great deal of research to be undertaken before concrete proposals can be made. One of the key barriers to funding research and exploration in this area is that a civilian population trained in methods of CBD would be able to use that capability against their own government if it tried to impose unpopular measures. This could make governments apprehensive, as it reduces their ability to force the population to obey.

Apart from providing an alternative means of national defence, CBD has a number of strengths and advantages. For example, abolishing the NZDF and adopting CBD instead would send a strong signal that Aotearoa was making itself unable to threaten invasion of, or attack against, any other nation, as CBD obviously cannot be used as an offensive tool of foreign policy. It would also signal that Aotearoa would not be fighting on the side of any Anglosphere-led wars in future either. This would contribute to wider disarmament efforts and reassure other nations that Aotearoa is no threat, either practically or symbolically. In turn, this would most likely have the effect of making Aotearoa less of a target of invasion or military or terrorist attack. Another advantage of CBD is that the decentralisation and diffusion of power not only protects against potential invasion, but makes the national defence system less vulnerable to non-traditional threats such as cyber-attack and espionage. CBD also has the advantage of involving ordinary citizens in the defence of the nation, thereby contributing to democracy and political participation in foreign affairs. Finally, as we will discuss later, abolishing the NZDF and adopting CBD would have great advantages in terms of resources that could be used for increasing human security, such as greater spending on health, welfare, education, climate adaptation, social justice and the like.

The Potential of Unarmed Civilian Peacekeeping

Given the importance of peacekeeping to Aotearoa's beliefs about the role of the NZDF, it is important to explore the possibilities of what has been termed unarmed civilian peacekeeping (UCP). There is growing empirical evidence for the potential of unarmed, nonviolent forms of peacekeeping – as opposed to using the armed forces of contributing nations as the United Nations does – to provide security and protection to civilians in situations of armed conflict. In fact, as we have already discussed, the NZDF's peacekeeping mission in Bougainville involved unarmed peacekeepers engaging in many of the activities that UCP advocates. It was a great success that clearly demonstrates how trusted unarmed peacekeepers can be highly effective, even in situations of armed conflict.

UCP involves groups of trained civilians, usually outsiders, employing forms of nonviolent action to protect local civilians from violence and the threat of violence, as well as to support local efforts to build peace.[23] UCP groups such as Nonviolent Peaceforce and Peace Brigades International explain that their roles involve activities

> ... including (but not limited to) accompaniment, presence, rumor control, community security meetings, securing safe passage, and monitoring. In every place where civilian peacekeeping is used around the world, it is always context specific; it is adapted and developed by the people who work on the ground.[24]

Importantly, rather than imposing external solutions based on a universal blueprint, these unarmed peacekeepers create safe or safer spaces for the various parties involved to come together, and 'allow the [local] parties themselves to determine the means and the terms of transforming/resolving the conflict'.[25]

UCP has operated in many conflict zones around the world, such as Guatemala, El Salvador, Colombia,

Sri Lanka, Nepal, Sudan, Indonesia, South Sudan and Georgia, among others, with surprisingly few fatalities among the peacekeepers and a great many documented successes.[26] These examples have shown that civilians in conflict zones can be protected from harm using nonviolent strategies, even when faced by hostile armed groups like rebels, soldiers and drug traffickers.[27] Interestingly, UCP developed as a form of conflict management at the same time that traditional peacekeeping became increasingly militarised.[28]

Additionally, being able to protect civilians without the use of violence or military force helps to break the cycle of violence within communities, because it involves consistent means and ends, trust-building and non-coercion, and does not reproduce the mechanism for violence by inserting more arms and the use of force into the situation. Empirical support for this kind of peace-keeping includes a study by researchers Kara Beckman and Kenneth B. Solberg which found that communities felt significantly safer and more secure when UCP was present.[29] Other research suggests that UCP reduces conflict-related deaths and deters violence, while Nonviolent Peaceforce's own research suggests that it is especially effective at protecting vulnerable women in conflict zones.[30] Other research shows that these projects can have a local-level impact within two years, but that it takes longer to become more established and have a larger, more strategic, impact.[31]

While more research is needed in this under-explored area, what has already been discovered and learned by UCP groups over decades of practice shows that there is real potential for nonviolent external intervention in conflicts. This means that it is perfectly reasonable to suggest that investing in UCP instead of the NZDF would be a worthwhile and valuable course of action with a great many potential benefits, especially in terms of the promotion of peace and security at the international level. At the very least, Aotearoa could meet its international obligations in this area without maintaining military forces. In fact, Aotearoa could potentially lead the world in the development of UCP, similar to the way it led the world in the anti-nuclear movement.

Alternative Spending to Create Security

In addition to the large sums that the New Zealand government currently spends on the NZDF, it is important to acknowledge the opportunity costs of military spending. In particular, putting large amounts of money towards the military can lead to the underfunding of crucial social institutions which are tasked with ensuring the safety and security of citizens – such as welfare, health and education systems, services for survivors of sexual and domestic violence, child poverty alleviation, violence reduction programmes, social housing, job training, international aid and development, disaster relief and combating climate change, among many others. Increasing resources to deal with these problems would be a tangible and measurable way of increasing the safety, security and wellbeing of society, and dollar for dollar, would most likely be a better investment in national security than the military.

As we have shown, militaries like the NZDF are extremely costly and consume a disproportionate amount of national and global resources which could be spent on services with more immediate and long-term benefits to society and security. The tension between military spending and social uplift was explicitly articulated by former US president Dwight D. Eisenhower in 1953 when speaking about the unfolding arms race between the United States and Soviet Union. In a famous speech, he said:

> Every gun that is made, every warship launched, every rocket fired signifies, in the final sense, a theft from those who hunger and are not fed, those who are cold and are not clothed. This world in arms is not spending money alone. It is spending the sweat of its laborers, the genius of its scientists, the hopes of its children.
>
> The cost of one modern heavy bomber is this: a modern brick school in more than 30 cities. It is two electric power plants, each serving a town of 60,000 population. It is two fine, fully equipped hospitals. It is some 50 miles of concrete highway. We pay for a single fighter plane with a half million bushels of wheat. We pay for a single destroyer with new homes that could have housed more than 8,000 people.[32]

Eisenhower's speech helps to demonstrate that military spending is not only wasteful, it is immoral – a kind of 'theft' from those whom the money could otherwise sustain. How a nation spends its money is not (or should not be) solely a matter of economic efficiency;

it is in fact, a statement of what a nation values. Even if military force were adequate for the defence of Aotearoa's territory, or an effective means of confronting terrorism and authoritarianism, it would still be questionable as to whether military spending could be justified while there is a need for social spending such as that described by Eisenhower. It becomes clear that this spending is not justifiable when we consider, as demonstrated above, that military force is not conducive to promoting stability and peace internationally, not sufficient for the territorial defence of Aotearoa and ill-suited to confronting major security challenges of the day, such as climate change.

A shocking and pertinent example of the wasteful nature of military spending is the recent upgrade of the *Te Kaha* and *Te Mana* frigates. Costing between \$600 and \$700 million, including \$140 million on top of the initial budget due to project management mistakes, the upgrade had the key goal of improving combat capabilities. The ability to work alongside countries such as the United States and United Kingdom was also highlighted. Speaking upon the return of *Te Mana* from Canada in 2022, where it had been for three years while the upgrades were carried out, Chief of Navy Rear Admiral David Proctor said:

> The ability to deliver the security outcomes that
> New Zealand wants is by working alongside higher end
> partners .... These ships – after the investment the
> government has made, represent a contemporary high
> end combat capability for New Zealand.[33]

The deal with Lockheed Martin Canada to upgrade the frigates was signed in 2014 and, in addition to the extra costs, experienced delays of three years, even prior to the Covid-19 pandemic. Eight years in the making, these expensive and prolonged upgrades were intended to extend the operational life of the frigates until around 2030, now only eight years away. One commentator questioned whether the years where the frigates weren't available would raise questions in government, particularly, Treasury, as to whether the frigates were truly needed. This is a perfectly reasonable question.[34]

Following Eisenhower's lead, let us briefly consider what else this and other military spending could go towards, or how it compares to spending in other areas that enhance the security and wellbeing of New Zealanders. One point of comparison could be the Crown settling Tiriti o Waitangi claims with iwi and hapū. Research has long established the plethora of social issues stemming from colonialism. Addressing New Zealand's colonial past and present is vital to developing a society that is equitable, and in which systemic barriers that inhibit people's autonomy are removed. Tiriti settlements alone are not sufficient for achieving this, but they are one well-known means of redress. Labelled as an iwi 'gravy train' by some, between 1975 and 2018 the total amount spent on settlements by the Crown was $2.24 billion.[35] These settlements, occurring over forty-three years, amount to just 272 days of defence spending, based on our current annual defence budget, and are less than the amount spent on the Poseidon planes alone, as discussed above. Iwi and hapū often invest the money they receive from Treaty settlements into education, businesses and conservation projects that benefit the broader community.

Another potential recipient of money currently being used on defence spending is our health system. Covid-19 merely highlighted what has always been true: a health system saves lives and is at the front line of ensuring the security and wellbeing of New Zealanders. Despite this, Aotearoa's health system has long been underfunded. This can be seen in the degradation of physical infra-structure, such as sewage leaks at Whangārei Hospital, or leaks following heavy rain at Dunedin Hospital, as well as in the undue pressure placed on under-staffed health workers.[36] The pandemic highlighted the heroic efforts of our healthcare workers, while also clarifying the shortcomings of the system in which they work. An outcome of New Zealand's underfunded health system is that healthcare becomes highly inequitable, as wealthy New Zealanders can afford to access private healthcare and avoid the outdated infrastructure and staffing shortages mentioned above.[37]

The high cost of building health infrastructure such as hospitals is often the main objection to such projects. That is, no one asserts that the people of Whangārei or Dunedin should live with inadequate hospital facilities. The decision of undertaking these large infrastructure projects is always framed as a matter of whether they can be afforded. As with all public spending, the required budget should be assessed as accurately as possible, and unnecessary spending should be minimised. Yet, there is a false economy to abandoning, delaying or underfunding these projects. As an anonymous commentator noted with regards to the redevelopment of Whangārei Hospital:

Of those 11 years [of the redevelopment], three of them will have been spent litigating and relitigating the decision. Much of those three years has been spent debating cost. This is a lot like deciding what to wear when the taxi's outside with the meter running, because construction costs keep rising. Since June 1994, inflation-adjusted construction prices – as measured by the PPI Construction Outputs Index – have never decreased on an annual basis . . . . If we don't have the money to pay for this increase in cost, then we have to find it. The alternative is the kind of value engineering Toffee Pops have undergone in the last give [sic] years. Sure, the price of Toffee Pops has remained relatively stable, but today's biscuit is a shadow of its former self – smaller and flatter and tasting of palm oil. This approach is distasteful for biscuits and objectionable for hospitals. We're talking about critically important buildings that deliver life or death services. Building undersized or ill-equipped hospitals misuses resources and places future population health at unnecessary risk.[38]

The redevelopment of Whangārei Hospital's main hospital block was initially budgeted at $572 million.[39] What the final cost will be is not known, as there are additional blocks of the hospital that require redevelopment and, as noted above, construction costs continue to rise. But put this in the context of the $600 to $700 million spent on the naval frigate upgrades. The projects are of similar costs. Both look like they might cost more than anticipated – the hospital due to unavoidable supply chain costs, the frigate upgrades due to project management mistakes. The frigate upgrades took eight years and have a shelf life of eight years. If invested in correctly, Whangārei Hospital should continue to serve the people of that region for decades to come. Moreover, while the money from the frigate upgrades went to Lockheed Martin Canada, an international arms company, hospital construction creates local jobs and stimulates the local economy. (The $1.47 billion Dunedin Hospital reconstruction, for example, is expected to create the equivalent of 1,000 full-time jobs and contribute $429 million to the local economy.[40]) Thus, while the frigate and Whangārei projects have comparable costs, the benefits to New Zealanders of the hospital redevelopment far outweigh those of the frigate upgrades.

We may also use examples from the international context. One Tomahawk cruise missile costs about US$2 million, enough to pay the annual salary of twenty-eight nurses in the United Kingdom health system. The Stockholm International Peace Research Institute calculated that global military expenditure in 2015 was US$1.7 trillion (by 2022 it was up to US$2.2 trillion) and that just 10 per cent of this could cover the costs of global goals aimed at ending poverty and hunger in fifteen years.[41] Certainly, if states had invested a few billion in their public health systems instead of the military, they might have been able to save a substantial number of the six and a half million lives lost to Covid-19 in the pandemic.

The central point is that if Aotearoa demilitarised, the current NZDF budget could be redistributed to areas such as civil defence forces that could be deployed locally and globally to respond to natural disasters and peacebuilding missions; nonviolent peacekeeping forces; building a social defence strategy; resources for nonviolent resistance movements; and putting more resources, both locally and globally, into areas that are currently underfunded but in reality are the first line of security in the lives of ordinary people, such as welfare, poverty reduction, climate change and social justice. In addition, more resources could go into research on nonviolent alternatives to the military, further enhancing its effectiveness.

Further, as well as the material costs of funding the NZDF, maintaining a military also involves costs to Aotearoa's reputation and leadership. Abolishing the military and diverting the resources into other areas could have potentially huge impacts on global norms and problem-solving. Seriously considering this idea offers a genuine opportunity for Aotearoa to be a peace leader in the world and to contribute in a major way to increased global security and innovative nonviolent solutions to increasingly complex security challenges. Becoming a world leader in nonviolent resistance training, UCP, social defence, peace diplomacy and conflict resolution would provide a wealth of potential benefits, both domestic and international.

Alternative Institutions for Alternative Military Roles

A common argument for maintaining the NZDF is that it is the only body in Aotearoa that has the capacity to respond to certain kinds of events, and it can play a useful role in responding to certain non-military threats. For example, the NZDF is frequently called upon to provide support for disaster relief, rescue, emergency transportation, fisheries protection, quarantine hotel security and the like. In recent years, alongside fisheries protection, the NZDF has been called upon to assist with the Christchurch and Kaikōura earthquakes, the Tonga tsunami, security for managed isolation facilities and more.

However, it seems reasonable to ask whether these types of roles could be more effectively dealt with by specialised agencies and groups, especially as we know that the NZDF's primary training and equipment is for war-fighting. There is also the issue that when the NZDF is on deployment overseas on a peacekeeping or military mission, it would be unable to participate in disaster relief, for example. It would seem to be much more efficient to have dedicated agencies that are specifically trained and equipped in disaster management, fisheries protection, search and rescue and so on.

Even in terms of other threats like cyber-attacks and terrorism, it is obvious that these issues cannot be dealt with using conventional military forces. Nullifying cyber-attacks, for example, requires technological solutions such as those sought by businesses in protecting customer information. This reality is reflected in the *National Plan to Address Cybercrime*, in which the NZDF is not listed as a government body having relevant roles or responsibilities.[42] The Ministry of Defence and NZDF do have some input into interagency bodies concerned with cyber-crime. However, the NZDF's responsibilities relate to securing their own operations from disruption, not the protection of national infrastructure.[43]

In other words, the argument that Aotearoa needs to retain the NZDF in order to deal with major disasters or patrol fishing zones or respond to cyber-attacks is unconvincing, unless the NZDF was completely reformed so that it was trained and equipped specifically for these tasks. The more effective and efficient option would be to abolish the NZDF and reassign these tasks to dedicated specialist units who are appropriately trained and resourced for the roles.

Small States without Armed Forces

Nations without militaries do exist. Most of them are states smaller than Aotearoa, such as Andorra and Iceland, as well as multiple island states in the Pacific and the Caribbean, such as Samoa or Dominica. However, Costa Rica and Panama, which have a similar population to New Zealand, also do not have militaries. On top of this, until fairly recently, Haiti, with a population of over 10 million people, spent over twenty years without a military. Reinstating it has proven contentious within the country. Domestic opponents to the change have argued that it will drain valuable resources and creates risks to the democratic process.[44] The multiple coups and instability Haiti has experienced were one reason for removing the military in the first place. The military forces were both unable to maintain law and order and more often were a cause of violence and instability.

Many of these smaller countries either removed their militaries or never formed militaries for reasons that align with many of the arguments that we have presented in this book. All have alternative organisations to deal with their internal security, law and order, marine protection and disaster management. Some have agreements with larger nations for their protection, such as Iceland (a NATO member), many Caribbean nations and Andorra. Others, such as Samoa, do not.[45]

Historically, states such as Haiti and Panama have seen first-hand the inability of their militaries to repel a superior military force. Raoul Cédras, leader of Haiti's military government between 1991 and 1994, resigned from leadership in 1994, recognising the inability of Haitian forces to repel the UN-backed US occupation that was to be mobilised were he to retain power. Similarly, Manuel Noriega of Panama was swiftly ousted from power despite Panamanian military efforts to resist US invasion in 1989.

Costa Rica is a particularly pertinent example of military abolition. It abolished its standing army in 1949 following a civil war and has remained free of large-scale violent internal conflict and external wars since. Its military budget was subsequently reallocated to security, welfare and culture, with extraordinary results. In 2017 the *Guardian* newspaper reported:

Every few years the New Economics Foundation publishes the Happy Planet Index – a measure of progress that looks at life expectancy, wellbeing and equality rather than the narrow metric of gross domestic product, and plots these measures against ecological impact. Costa Rica tops the list of countries every time. With a life expectancy of 79.1 years and levels of wellbeing in the top 7 per cent of the world, Costa Rica matches many Scandinavian nations in these areas and neatly outperforms the United States. And it manages all of this with a GDP per capita of only $10,000 (£7,640), less than one fifth that of the US. In this sense, Costa Rica is the most efficient economy on earth: it produces high standards of living with low GDP and minimal pressure on the environment.[46]

The article went on to suggest that this extraordinary success was due to Costa Rica's commitment to universalism:

[T]he principle that everyone – regardless of income – should have equal access to generous, high-quality social services as a basic right. A series of progressive governments started rolling out healthcare, education and social security in the 1940s and expanded these to the whole population from the 1950s onward, *after abolishing the military and freeing up more resources for social spending.*[47]

Costa Rica's commitment to universalism contrasts to the approach of successive New Zealand governments since the neoliberal economic reforms of the 1980s. Instead, Aotearoa has seen privatisation and reduction in public funding for social services at the same time as there has been continuing high per capita levels of military funding. The example of Costa Rica suggests that abolishing the NZDF could be politically feasible, in part because it would be beneficial to the long-term security, society and environment of Aotearoa, particularly if it was accompanied by a similar shift to universalism.

Summary

In this chapter, we have explored some of the main alternatives to military force for tasks like national defence, peacekeeping, disaster response and more. We have demonstrated that the argument that there are no alternatives to maintaining military forces is much more a myth than reality. This myth is based on ignorance about the history and potential of civilian-based defence, unarmed civilian peacekeeping, examples like Costa Rica and the nature of the NZDF itself, which is trained and equipped primarily for war-fighting.

The arguments and evidence we have presented in this chapter provide good reasons for the country to seriously consider abolishing the NZDF. Further, they are a useful starting point for thinking about how we might continue to be involved in international peacekeeping, how we might rethink Aotearoa's role on the international stage as a peace leader and how we might think about reorganising for tasks like disaster relief, fisheries protection, responding to cyber-attacks and so on. There are no real practical or conceptual obstacles, apart from a mindset stuck in the myths of the past, to replacing the NZDF with new institutions dedicated to nonviolent approaches, like CBD and UCP. The knowledge and experience to draw upon already exists, including those in the NZDF who participated in the Bougainville mission.

Conclusion
Replacing Myth with Reality

When all the evidence and arguments for abolishing the New Zealand Defence Force are put together in one place, we believe that they make a compelling case for seriously considering such a radical option, and that such an option should be debated widely in the public arena. This is particularly true at those times when there is a review of the country's national security system, as occurred in early 2023 when we were completing this book. Moreover, the debate needs to take place in a realistic, sober and informed way, rather than on the basis of misleading, if comforting, myths. This is why we structured our book as an interrogation of the dominant myths about the NZDF in Aotearoa New Zealand. It was never our intention to provide a foolproof argument for why we should abolish the New Zealand Defence Force – no such argument exists or likely could exist – but instead to invite further discussion. We seek to start – or perhaps to continue – a conversation which challenges the 'common sense' logic which argues that in Aotearoa New Zealand there is no alternative to the maintenance of a national military.

At the same time, we recognise that the abolition of the NZDF and a move to alternative nonviolent methods of national defence and peacekeeping would involve some unknowns and some risks. As with Aotearoa's radical decision to ban nuclear ship visits in 1984, it could result in a deterioration in our relationships with former defence partners and allies. It could have economic costs in relation to free trade agreements if powerful states decided to punish us for the move. It could lead to some loss of influence in the Pacific or increased diplomatic pressure from China, Russia or other belligerent powers. And it could have an impact on the communities within Aotearoa who find employment and a life of service in the NZDF. Or it could lead to the opposite – widespread respect, greater moral and political influence, new employment and community service pathways, and increased security as a neutral, peaceful, decolonised nation.

Either way, abolishing the NZDF would certainly require far more planning and research to make it a reality than has been, or could be, included in this book. We do not see this book as a detailed blueprint or practical handbook for action, but an effort to point out that nonviolent alternatives exist, they work and they would likely have a great many positive benefits, even if some of them are still at an embryotic stage of development. Nevertheless, there is something practical we could do in response right now. At the very least, in light of the arguments put forward in this book, we could as a nation choose to immediately end our involvement in military operations overseas, stop recruiting young people to join the military and substantially reduce the NZDF budget. These resources could instead be used to increase and fulfil our currently pitiable refugee quota, fund a well-run public health system, end child poverty, take major steps in climate change mitigation, fund social cohesion initiatives, strengthen disaster management bodies and so on. These are steps we could take today which would allow us to begin the journey towards a more positive role in international peace and security, decolonising our society and greater national wellbeing. The key point is that the lack of a detailed blueprint or handbook should not be taken as a reason to put off a decision or refuse to debate the issue in good faith.

Of course, this is not the only objection to our proposal. There are those who would argue that we should not consider such a course of action because New Zealand would lose influence and the benefits that come with our alliances and active participation in international operations. As we have contended in this book, this argument requires close scrutiny and an honest accounting to assess its merits. What exactly are the benefits that accrue from alliance participation, and are they outweighed by the costs? Are any economic benefits of alliance involvement worth the expensive investment of the NZDF? Are there alternative ways of gaining such economic benefits that don't involve military alliance participation? Does our participation, particularly in Anglosphere wars, actually increase the threat to Aotearoa, and would our security be enhanced by neutrality, for example? If this participation provides such important benefits, why does Aotearoa continue to adhere to its nuclear-free status which is an obstacle to even greater levels of participation? We suggest that an honest and forthright accounting of this objection would suggest that while there are some risks and potential costs to abolishing the NZDF, they are most likely outweighed by the potential benefits that could come from demilitarisation and neutrality.

Another common objection is that Aotearoa has a duty as a good international citizen to contribute to United Nations and other peace support operations and military interventions. In Chapters 3 and 4, we explored this argument and found it wanting. It's a myth. There's very little evidence that such operations really work to benefit the countries they take place in or increase international peace and security, and in fact approaches like unarmed civilian peacekeeping provide more effective, non-military options. In any case, the NZDF has been slowly transitioning away from peacekeeping and engaging more often in wars waged by its Anglosphere allies.

But what about China, Russia or aggressive nations who might emerge in the future, others will object. Don't we need the NZDF to protect our territory and territorial waters from military threats? Again, as we have tried to demonstrate in this book, this objection is weak, not least because the NZDF, as the military of a small state, does not have the capacity to protect Aotearoa against invasion. Moreover, the NZDF itself views this threat as being remote. A stronger argument here is that if we abolished the NZDF and could not therefore contribute to our alliance partners, they would not come to our defence in the event that a hostile power did decide to invade Aotearoa. Once again, however, such an argument needs scrutiny. There are reasons for thinking that not only would such a scenario lead to immense destruction of the land and people of Aotearoa, but also that our alliance partners might not be willing to risk nuclear confrontation over a small Pacific island, particularly one that already had broken our primary defence agreement by going nuclear free. There is also the question of whether this is a zero-sum game or whether we could pursue security in other ways – through strict neutrality or the development of a peace leader reputation, for example.

A more emotionally powerful argument against abolishing the NZDF is that Aotearoa's national identity and its Anzac-defined political culture makes the military essential to nation-building. This is certainly true and abolishing the NZDF would have to be accompanied by a renewed national narrative and set of public rituals which reaffirm our values and identity. Making the change would be difficult and painful and would no doubt face enormous opposition from large sections of the public and the political elite. However, it should not be ruled out simply because the military has historically played this role. The truth is that Aotearoa has more than one kind of national tradition. It also has a strong historical peace tradition which includes the Moriori peace covenant in Rēkohu, the Parihaka community's nonviolent resistance to colonial conquest, the conscientious objection movement in World War 1, the anti-Vietnam War protest movement and the anti-nuclear movement, among others. As often as ordinary New Zealanders have volunteered to fight in the military or support it in remembrance rituals, just as many have mobilised to oppose war and violence. Arguably, Aotearoa's national identity today is as much defined by its peacemaking and anti-nuclear traditions as it is by its involvement in past wars and military adventures.[1] These peace traditions are rooted in both Māori and Pākehā culture and values, and they could become the foundation for a new national identity, one that doesn't revolve around the NZDF and Anzac commemorations.

Crucially, abolishing the NZDF could also be seen as an important symbolic step towards acknowledging the harm suffered by Māori during colonisation, including the harm to Māori service personnel since then, and the forging of a decolonial society based on Te Tiriti partnership. The connections between defence approaches and colonisation, and ways to transcend their past wrongs, have been highlighted most recently by Te Pāti Māori's proposed defence policy, discussed in Chapter 1.

A final argument against abolishing the NZDF is that it is not politically possible. The proposition is too radical for the current political climate, especially after Russia invaded Ukraine in 2022 and there seemed to be no alternative to armed resistance by the Ukrainians. This is a compelling point, and hard to deny. There are few real pacifists in the world today, and few nations are willing to reduce their military spending, much less disarm. Nevertheless, we would argue that this observation should not prevent us from having an honest and rigorous public debate about the issue. After all, things that are 'politically impossible' can later become possible, in part through informed debate and argument. It was once deemed politically impossible that women be allowed to vote, that the Iron Curtain would fall, that apartheid would end and Nelson Mandela be released, or that governments would spend trillions of dollars on public health measures and economic rehabilitation in response to a health crisis.

In fact, the response to the Covid-19 pandemic has redefined what is politically possible as states have made enormous and radical changes and investments that would have been seen as politically impossible in the years before the pandemic. We suggest that just as the government listened to the evidence and arguments put forward by public health scientists in how to respond to the pandemic, the government similarly takes note of the evidence and arguments for abolishing the NZDF. Aotearoa New Zealand has a new political reality after the pandemic, one in which research and evidence play a key role in the making of public policy. We would argue that such an approach needs to be adopted in relation to the NZDF, too. The politically impossible is also being made possible today in other areas – most notably our response to the climate crisis. Perhaps as part of that response, we might seriously consider abolishing the NZDF for its net contribution to climate change.

In the end, the politically possible is defined and acted upon by people who make it happen; things become politically possible when people make them so. Academics such as ourselves, and a large number of peace activists and movements, believe that it is politically possible to abolish the NZDF, reorient Aotearoa's role to that of peacemaker and begin to adopt alternative nonviolent forms of national defence and international involvement. We believe it is high time this proposition is seriously debated in the public arena.

Notes

1. The Myth of the New Zealand Defence Force

1   Ministry of Defence, *Defence Assessment 2014*, Wellington, 2015, p.25, www.defence.govt.nz/assets/Uploads/802ce528c8/defence-assessment-2014-public.pdf (accessed 7 October 2022).

2   Ministry of Defence, *Defence Assessment 2021: He Moana Pukepuke e Ekengia e te Waka / A Rough Sea Can Still Be Navigated*, Wellington, 2021, p.22, www.defence.govt.nz/assets/publication/file/Defence-Assessment-2021.pdf (accessed 7 October 2022).

3   Australian Government Department of Defence, *2020 Defence Strategic Update*, 1 July 2020, www.defence.gov.au/about/strategic-planning/2020-defence-strategic-update (accessed 19 April 2023).

4   See Jacinda Ardern's description of the Indo-Pacific region in her 14 July 2021 speech to the New Zealand Institute of International Affairs. A transcript of the speech can be found at: www.beehive.govt.nz/release/prime-ministers-speech-nziia-annual-conference (accessed 6 October 2022).

5   Ministry of Defence, *Defence Assessment 2021*, p.14.

6   Ibid., pp.15, 23.

7   Ibid., p.15.

8   Ministry of Defence, *The Climate Crisis: Defence Readiness and Responsibilities*, Wellington, 2018, p.3, www.defence.govt.nz/assets/Uploads/66cfc96a20/Climate-Change-and-Security-2018.pdf (accessed 7 October 2022).

9   Ministry of Defence, *Defence Assessment 2021*, p.16.

10 Ibid., p.19.

11 Ibid., p.15.

12 Ibid., p.23.

13 Ibid.

14 Ministry of Defence, *The Climate Crisis*, p.3.

15 Ministry of Defence, *Defence Assessment 2021*, p.15.

16 'Ā Mātau Tangata, Mō Mātou Ngā Turanga: Our People, Structure and Leadership', New Zealand Defence Force Te Ope Kātua o Aotearoa (NZDF), www.nzdf.mil.nz/nzdf/our-people-structure-and-leadership (accessed 14 July 2023).

17 See the National Material Capabilities (version 6.0) dataset:

https://correlatesofwar.org/data-sets/national-material-capabilities (accessed 6 October 2022).

18   NZDF, *Statement of Intent 2015–2018*, Wellington, 2015, p.10, www.nzdf.mil.nz/downloads/pdf/public-docs/nzdf_soi_2015. pdf (accessed 15 August 2017); and NZDF, *The 2021/22–2024/25 Statement of Intent Tauākī Whakamaunga Atu*, Wellington, 2022, p.10, www.nzdf.mil.nz/assets/Uploads/DocumentLibrary/NZDF-Statement-of-Intent-2021-2024.PDF (accessed 14 July 2023).

19   NZDF, *Statement of Intent 2015–2018*, p.6.

20   Ministry of Defence, *Strategic Defence Policy Statement 2018*, Wellington, July 2018, p.35, www.defence.govt.nz/assets/ Uploads/8958486b29/Strategic-Defence-Policy-Statement-2018. pdf (accessed 7 October 2022).

21   NZDF website, www.nzdf.mil.nz/army (accessed 6 October 2022); and NZ Army Ngati Tumatauenga, *Army25: Chief of Army's Brief*, p.11, www.nzdf.mil.nz/assets/Uploads/DocumentLibrary/ Army-2025-booklet-spread-v2.pdf (accessed 13 July 2023).

22   NZDF, *2018/19–2021/22 Statement of Intent*, Wellington, 2018, www.nzdf.mil.nz/assets/Uploads/DocumentLibrary/NZDF-Statement-of-Intent-2018-2021-1.pdf; and NZDF, *The 2021/22–2024/25 Statement of Intent*.

23   Ministry of Defence, *Defence Assessment 2021*, p.30.

24   Figures from Stockholm International Peace Research Institute's military expenditure database. The data can be browsed at https://milex.sipri.org/sipri (accessed 7 October 2022) and at the World Bank, https://data.worldbank.org/indicator/MS.MIL. XPND.CN?locations=NZ (accessed 26 July 2023).

25   The World Bank, 'Military Expenditure (% of GDP) – New Zealand', https://data.worldbank.org/indicator/MS.MIL. XPND.GD.ZS?locations=NZ (accessed 26 July 2023).

26   The Treasury, *Vote Defence Force*, Wellington, 2021, p.46, www. treasury.govt.nz/publications/estimates/vote-defence-force-external-sector-estimates-2021-22 (accessed 7 October 2022).

27   NZDF, *2021 NZDF Annual Report*, Wellington, 2021, p.96, www. nzdf.mil.nz/assets/Uploads/DocumentLibrary/M21-038-NZDF-Annual-Report-2021-WEB.pdf (accessed 7 October 2022).

28   'Equipment and Technology' section of the NZDF's Defence Careers website, www.defencecareers.mil.nz/army/lifestyle-salary/equipment-and-technology (accessed 3 May 2018).

29   New Zealand Army Ngāti Tūmatauenga, 'Ā Mātou Taputapu: Our Equipment', NZDF, www.nzdf.mil.nz/army/our-equipment (accessed 13 July 2023).

30   Ministry of Defence, *Major Projects Report 2020*, 2020, www. defence.govt.nz/assets/publication/file/MPR-2020.pdf (accessed 13 July 2023).

31   Ibid., p.19.

32   Laura Walters, 'Submarine-Hunting Planes to Replace
      Ageing Orions', Stuff, 9 July 2018, www.stuff.co.nz/national/
      politics/105338789/submarinehunting-planes-to-replace-
      ageing-orions (accessed 10 October 2022).

33   Bethan Greener, 'The New Zealand Defence Force Role in
      New Zealand Foreign Policy', in Anne-Marie Brady (ed.), *Small
      States and the Changing Global Order: New Zealand Faces the
      Future*, Springer, Cham, 2019.

34   Nicky Hager, 'Principled Small Nation or Stalwart Ally?
      New Zealand's Independent Foreign Policy', in Brady (ed.), *Small
      States and the Changing Global*.

35   Ibid.

36   Jacinda Ardern, speech to the New Zealand Institute of
      International Affairs, 14 July 2021.

37   Nanaia Mahuta, speech to the New Zealand Institute of
      International Affairs, 3 November 2021. A transcript of the
      speech can be found at: www.beehive.govt.nz/speech/aotearoa-
      new%C2%A0zealand's-pacific-engagement-partnering-
      resilience (accessed 10 August 2023).

38   NZDF, *NZDF Strategic Plan 2019–2025: Operationalising
      Strategy25*, p.8, www.nzdf.mil.nz/assets/Uploads/
      DocumentLibrary/NZDF-Strategic-Plan-2019-2025-v2.pdf
      (accessed 17 October 2022).

39   Will Trafford, 'Māori Party Adopts Swiss Neutrality Policy', Te Ao
      Māori News, 9 February 2023, www.teaonews.co.nz/2023/02/09/
      maori-party-adopts-swiss-neutrality-policy (accessed
      26 July 2023).

40   Ibid.

41   Green Party of Aotearoa and New Zealand, *Defence and
      Peacekeeping Policy*, version of 11 April 2023, https://assets.
      nationbuilder.com/beachheroes/pages/9641/attachments/
      original/1682560097/Policy-Greens_Defence-and-
      Peacekeeping-Policy-2011-2023.pdf?1682560097 (accessed
      26 July 2023).

42   Green Party of Aotearoa and New Zealand, *Defence and
      Peacekeeping Policy*, 2020, https://assets.nationbuilder.com/
      beachheroes/pages/9641/attachments/original/1591177490/
      Policy-Greens_Defence_and_Peacekeeping.pdf?1591177490
      (accessed 10 October 2022).

43   Te Pāti Māori, 'Te Pāti Māori Announce Military Neutrality
      as New Transformative Defence Policy', press release,
      Scoop, 4 February 2023, www.scoop.co.nz/stories/PO2302/
      S00034/te-pati-maori-announce-military-neutrality-as-new-
      transformative-defence-policy.htm (accessed 26 July 2023).

44   NZDF, *2021 NZDF Annual Report*, Wellington, 2021, p.116, www.
      nzdf.mil.nz/assets/Uploads/DocumentLibrary/M21-038-NZDF-
      Annual-Report-2021-WEB.pdf (accessed 7 October 2022).
      Further information on specific deployments is drawn from
      the Ministry of Defence's *2020 Briefing to Incoming Minister of
      Defence*, which is available at: www.defence.govt.nz/the-latest/
      story/bim-2020 (accessed 10 October 2022), and the Ministry
      of Defence's 'Deployments Map', which can be found at: www.
      defence.govt.nz/what-we-do/diplomacy-and-deployments/
      deployment-map (accessed 10 October 2022).
45   See the Combined Maritime Forces Twitter bio: https://twitter.
      com/CMF_Bahrain?ref_src=twsrc%5Etfw%7Ctwcamp%5E-
      embeddedtimeline%7Ctwterm%5Escreen-name%3ACMF_
      Bahrain%7Ctwcon%5Es1_c1 (accessed 10 October 2022).
46   Ministry of Defence, 'Deployments Map'.
47   Ministry of Defence, *2020 Briefing to Incoming Minister of
      Defence*, 2020.
48   Kurt Bayer, 'Taliban Welcomes NZDF Withdrawal from
      Afghanistan after 20 Years', *New Zealand Herald*, 18 February 2021,
      www.nzherald.co.nz/nz/taliban-welcomes-nzdf-withdrawal-from-
      afghanistan-after-20-years/SMU542NJUTOVCMKPWCXH-
      WAAV5M (accessed 10 October 2022).
49   The Treasury, *Vote Defence Force*, Wellington, 2021, p.46,
      www.treasury.govt.nz/publications/estimates/vote-defence-force-
      external-sector-estimates-2021-22 (accessed 7 October 2022).
50   NZDF, *Annual Report 2019*, Wellington, 2019, www.nzdf.mil.nz/
      assets/Uploads/DocumentLibrary/NZDF-Annual-Report-2019-
      1.pdf (accessed 10 October 2022).
51   Ministry of Defence, 'Deployments Map'.
52   'Fiji Aid Operation Prepares for Exit', Radio New Zealand,
      17 April 2016, *www.rnz.co.nz/news/national/301717/fiji-aid-
      operation-prepares-for-exit (accessed 14 August 2023)*.
53   Ministry of Defence, *Strategic Defence Policy Statement 2018*.
54   Ibid.
55   Laura Walters, 'New Sub-killer Planes May Never Fire in Anger
      but Govt Wants the Option', Stuff, 14 July 2018, www.stuff.co.nz/
      national/politics/105452173/new-subkiller-planes-may-never-
      fire-in-anger-but-govt-wants-the-option (accessed 10 October
      2022).
56   See Aotearoa's National Civil Defence Emergency Management
      Plan Order 2015, www.legislation.govt.nz/regulation/public/
      2015/0140/latest/whole.html (accessed 11 October 2022).
57   Henry L. Roediger III and Magdalena Abel, 'Collective Memory:
      A New Arena of Cognitive Study', *Trends in Cognitive Sciences*, 19,
      7 (2015), p.359.

58   Ernest Renan, 'What Is a Nation?', in J.K. Olick, V. Vinitzky-
      Seroussi and D. Levy (eds), *The Collective Memory Reader*, Oxford
      University Press, Oxford, 2011, p.80.
59   Vincent O'Malley, *The New Zealand Wars | Ngā Pakanga o
      Aotearoa*, Bridget Williams Books, Wellington, 2019.
60   Benedict Anderson, *Imagined Communities: Reflections on the
      Origin and Spread of Nationalism*, Verso, London 1991, p.9.
61   John Bevan-Smith, 'Gallipoli: Remembrance as Forgetting',
      Scoop, 22 February 2015, www.scoop.co.nz/stories/HL1502/
      S00138/gallipoli-remembrance-as-forgetting-john-bevan-smith.
      htm (accessed 11 October 2022).
62   Chris Maclean and Jock Phillips, *The Sorrow and the Pride:
      New Zealand War Memorials*, Historical Branch and GP Books,
      Wellington, 1990, p.71.
63   Ministry for Culture and Heritage, 'Anzac Day Activities',
      New Zealand Histories, updated 29 March 2022, https://
      nzhistory.govt.nz/page/anzac-day-activities (accessed 11 October
      2022).
64   See Tracy Watkins, 'Anzac Force Mooted for Iraq Deployment',
      Stuff, 1 December 2014, www.stuff.co.nz/national/
      politics/63722810/anzac-force-mooted-for-iraq-deployment
      (accessed 11 October 2022), and Tracy Watkins and Vernon Small,
      'Anzac Troop Move Slammed by Labour', Stuff, 2 December 2014,
      www.stuff.co.nz/national/politics/63729670/anzac-troop-move-
      slammed-by-labour (accessed 11 October 2022).

2. The Myth of National Security

1   Columba Peoples and Nick Vaughan-Williams, *Critical Security
      Studies: An Introduction*, 3rd edn, Routledge, Abingdon, 2020.
2   Barry Buzan, Ole Wæver and Jaap de Wilde, *Security: A New
      Framework for Analysis*, Lynne Rienner, Boulder, CO, 1998.
3   World Health Organization, 'WHO Coronavirus (COVID-19)
      Dashboard: Overview', updated 12 July 2023, https://covid19.
      who.int (accessed 17 July 2023).
4   Ken Booth, *Theory of World Security*, Cambridge University
      Press, Cambridge, 2007, p.102.
5   New Zealand Government, *Defence White Paper 2016*, p.17, www.
      defence.govt.nz/assets/Uploads/daac08133a/defence-white-
      paper-2016.pdf (accessed 17 October 2022).
6   Data available at the Uppsala Conflict Data Program, Department
      of Peace and Conflict research, Uppsala University, https://ucdp.
      uu.se (accessed 17 October 2022).
7   Håvard Strand, Siri Aas Rustad, Henrik Urdal and Håvard
      Mokleiv Nygård, 'Trends in Armed Conflict, 1946–2018', *Conflict

Trends, 3 (2019), PRIO, Oslo, www.prio.org/publications/11349 (accessed 14 August 2023).

8   Notably, the conflict in Iraq was not counted as a war within PRIO's research that year, as battle-related deaths dipped from close to 10,000 in 2017, to 831 in 2018. The researchers noted that similar dips were seen in certain calendar years since the 2003 invasion and that a return to war in Iraq should not be ruled out.

9   Håvard Strand and Håvard Hegre, 'Trends in Armed Conflict, 1946–2020', *Conflict Trends*, 3 (2021), PRIO, Oslo, www.prio.org/publications/12756 (accessed 26 July 2023).

10 Dustin Ells Howes, 'The Failure of Pacifism and the Success of Nonviolence', *Perspectives on Politics*, 11, 2 (2013), p.433.

11 See Stephen Biddle, *Military Power: Explaining Victory and Defeat in Modern Battle*, Princeton University Press, Princeton, NJ, 2004; see Ivan Arreguín-Toft, *How the Weak Win Wars: A Theory of Asymmetric Conflict*, Cambridge University Press, New York, 2005.

12 See Alexei Anisin, 'Violence Begets Violence: Why States Should Not Lethally Repress Popular Protest', *The International Journal of Human Rights*, 20, 7 (2016), pp.893–913.

13 Molly Wallace, *Security without Weapons: Rethinking Violence, Nonviolent Action, and Civilian Protection*, Routledge, Abingdon, 2016.

14 Evan Perkoski and Erica Chenoweth, 'Nonviolent Resistance and Prevention of Mass Killings During Popular Uprisings', *ICNC Special Report Series*, 2 (April 2018), www.nonviolent-conflict.org/wp-content/uploads/2017/07/nonviolent-resistance-and-prevention-of-mass-killings-perkoski-chenoweth-2018-icnc.pdf (accessed 18 October 2022).

15 See Javier Argomaniz and Alberto Vidal-Diez, 'Examining Deterrence and Backlash Effects in Counter-Terrorism: The Case of ETA', *Terrorism and Political Violence*, 27, 1 (2015), pp.160–81.

16 See Darius Rejali, *Torture and Democracy*, Princeton University Press, Princeton, NJ, 2009; and Laurie Calhoun, *We Kill because We Can: From Soldiering to Assassination in the Drone Age*, Zed Books, London, 2015.

17 See Max Abrahms, 'Why Terrorism Does Not Work', *International Security*, 31, 2 (2006), pp.42–78; and Erica Chenoweth and Maria J. Stephan, *Why Civil Resistance Works: The Strategic Logic of Nonviolent Conflict*, Columbia University Press, New York, 2011.

18 See Charles Anderton and Edward Ryan, 'Habituation to Atrocity: Low-Level Violence against Civilians as a Predictor of High-Level Attacks', *Journal of Genocide Research*, 18, 4 (2016), http://dx.doi.org/10.1080/14623528.2016.1216109; and Barbara

Walter, 'Does Conflict Beget Conflict? Explaining Recurring Civil War', *Journal of Peace Research*, 41, 3 (2004), pp.371–88.

19   See Richard English, *Modern War: A Very Short Introduction*, Oxford University Press, Oxford, 2013.

20   For discussions on this, see Todd May, *Nonviolent Resistance: A Philosophical Introduction*, Polity, Cambridge, 2015, pp.49–52; and Richard Jackson, 'Pacifism: The Anatomy of a Subjugated Knowledge', *Critical Studies on Security*, 6, 2, (2018), pp.160–75.

21   See Wallace, *Security without Weapons*.

22   This point is firmly illustrated through an analysis of three major cases where violent state suppression of political groups resulted not in surrender but increased violent resistance in Eitan Alimi, Chares Demetriou and Lorenzo Bosi, *The Dynamics of Radicalization: A Relational and Comparative Perspective*, Oxford University Press, Oxford, 2015, pp.242–46.

23   Howes, 'The Failure of Pacifism', p.436.

24   Stellan Vinthagen, *A Theory of Nonviolent Action: How Civil Resistance Works*, Zed Books, London, 2015, pp.193–94.

25   Hannah Arendt, *On Violence*, Harcourt, Brace & World, New York, 1970, p.56.

26   Mahatma Gandhi, *The Collected Works of Gandhi: Volume 31*, Publications Division Government of India, New Delhi, 1999, p.372, www.gandhiashramsevagram.org/gandhi-literature/collected-works-of-mahatma-gandhi-volume-1-to-98.php (accessed 26 July 2023).

27   Arendt, *On Violence*, p.80.

28   For more in-depth discussion of these arguments, see Richard Jackson, 'A Pacifist Critique of Just War Theory', in Luís Cordeiro-Rodrigues and Danny Singh (eds), *Comparative Just War Theory*, Rowman & Littlefield, Lanham, ML, 2020, pp.45–60; and Richard Jackson, 'Pacifism and the Ethical Imagination in IR', *International Politics*, 56, 2 (2019), https://doi.org/10.1057/s41311-017-0137-6, pp.212–27.

29   See the 'Costs of War' figures produced by the Watson Institute for International and Public Affairs at Brown University: https://watson.brown.edu/costsofwar/figures/2021/WarDeathToll (accessed 12 October 2022).

30   See Physicians for Social Responsibility, 'Body Count: Casualty Figures after 10 Years of the "War on Terror"', March 2015, https://psr.org/wp-content/uploads/2018/05/body-count.pdf (accessed 18 October 2022).

31   Freedom House, *Freedom in the World 2020: A Leaderless Struggle for Democracy*, 2020, https://freedomhouse.org/sites/default/files/2020-02/FIW_2020_REPORT_BOOKLET_Final.pdf (accessed 17 October 2022).

32 Among a large literature detailing the effects of the war on terror, see Tom Parker, *Avoiding the Terrorist Trap: Why Respect for Human Rights Is the Key to Defeating Terrorism*, World Scientific Publishing Europe Ltd, London, 2019.

33 Hannah Ritchie, Joe Hasell, Edouard Mathieu, Cameron Appel and Max Roser, 'Terrorism', Our World in Data, first published 2013, revised 2022, https://ourworldindata.org/terrorism (accessed 12 October 2022).

34 Ibid. For more statistics and discussion of the threat posed by terrorism, see also John Mueller and Mark G. Stewart, 'Terrorism and Bathtubs: Comparing and Assessing the Risks', *Terrorism and Political Violence*, 33, 1 (2021), https://doi.org/10.1080/09546553.2018.1530662, pp.138–63; and Robert Goodin, *What's Wrong with Terrorism?*, Polity, Cambridge, 2006.

35 Chris Bosley, 'Violent Extremist Disengagement and Reconciliation: A Peacebuilding Approach', Peaceworks, no. 163, July 2020, www.usip.org/publications/2020/07/violent-extremist-disengagement-and-reconciliation-peacebuilding-approach (accessed 18 October 2022).

36 Intergovernmental Panel on Climate Change, *Global Warming of 1.5°C: Special Report*, IPCC, 2018, www.ipcc.ch/sr15 (accessed 17 July 2023).

37 Intergovernmental Science-Policy Platform on Biodiversity and Ecosystem Services, *Global Assessment Report on Biodiversity and Ecosystem Services*, 6 May 2019, https://ipbes.net/global-assessment (accessed 17 October 2022).

38 DARA, *Climate Vulnerability Monitor*, 2nd edn, 2012, http://daraint.org/climate-vulnerability-monitor/climate-vulnerability-monitor-2012 (accessed 18 October 2022).

39 See International Crisis Group, 'Climate, Environment and Conflict', www.crisisgroup.org/future-conflict/climate-environment-and-conflict (accessed 18 October 2022).

40 Kanta Kumari Rigaud, Alex de Sherbinin, Bryan Jones, Jonas Bergmann, Viviane Clement, Kayly Ober, Jacob Schewe, Susana Adamo, Brent McCusker, Silke Heuser and Amelia Midgley, *Groundswell: Preparing for Internal Climate Migration*, World Bank, Washington, DC, 2018, https://openknowledge.worldbank.org/handle/10986/29461 (accessed 18 October 2022).

41 Among a large literature, see Jonathan Goodhand, 'Enduring Disorder and Persistent Poverty: A Review of the Linkages between War and Chronic Poverty', *World Development*, 31, 3 (2003), pp.629–46; Richard Jackson, 'The State and Internal Conflict', *Australian Journal of International Affairs*, 55, 1 (2001), pp.65–81; and Thomas Homer-Dixon, 'Environmental Scarcities

and Violent Conflict: Evidence from Cases', *International Security*, 19, 1 (1994), pp.5–40.

42   Institute for Policy Studies, *The Military and Climate Change*, 2020, https://ips-dc.org/wp-content/uploads/2020/06/No-Warming-No-War_02-Military-and-Climate-Change.pdf (accessed 18 October 2020).

43   Emalani Case, 'Dear New Zealand, Please Don't Bring Your War Games to My Hawaiian Home', The Spinoff, 10 June 2020, https://thespinoff.co.nz/politics/10-06-2020/dear-new-zealand-please-dont-bring-your-war-games-to-my-hawaiian-home (accessed 3 April 2023).

3. The Myth of the 'Good International Citizen'

1   David Capie, 'Peacekeeping – New Zealand's Involvement in Peacekeeping', 2012, Te Ara – the Encyclopedia of New Zealand, www.TeAra.govt.nz/en/peacekeeping/page-1 (accessed 12 October 2022); Audrey Young, 'NZ Has Avoided United Nations Peacekeeping Missions because of Safety Concerns: McCully', *New Zealand Herald*, 5 April 2017, www.nzherald.co.nz/nz/nz-has-avoided-united-nations-peacekeeping-missions-because-of-safety-concerns-mccully/IOAZKA6MZ7BUJ3T-5GK23RANG3Y/#:~:text=The%20Government%20has%20avoided%20significant,minister%20Murray%20McCully%20has%20revealed (accessed 12 October 2022).

2   Nicky Hager and Jon Stephenson, *Hit and Run: The New Zealand SAS in Afghanistan and the Meaning of Honour*, Potton & Burton, Nelson, 2017.

3   Capie, 'Peacekeeping'.

4   Ibid.

5   United Nations, *Panel on United Nations Peace Operations*, 2000, https://documents-dds-ny.un.org/doc/UNDOC/GEN/N00/594/70/PDF/N0059470.pdf?OpenElement (accessed 12 October 2022).

6   Bethan Greener, 'Peacekeeping Contributor Profile: New Zealand', *Providing for Peacekeeping*, 2015, www.providingforpeacekeeping.org/2014/04/03/contributor-profile-new-zealand (accessed 2 November 2017).

7   Ibid.

8   Young, 'NZ Has Avoided United Nations Peacekeeping Missions'.

9   Capie, 'Peacekeeping'.

10   There is a large literature pointing out the failures of UN peacekeeping and peacebuilding. See among many others: Michael Pugh, 'The Political Economy of Peacebuilding: A Critical Theory Perspective', *International Journal of Peace*

Studies, 10, 2 (2005), pp.23–42; Neil Cooper, 'Review Article: On the Crisis of the Liberal Peace', *Conflict, Security and Development*, 7, 4 (2007), pp.605–16; Oliver Richmond, 'Failed Statebuilding versus Peace Formation', *Cooperation and Conflict*, 48, 3 (2013), pp.378–400.

11 Information on the NZDF's work in Timor-Leste sourced from Steven Ratuva and Anne-Marie Brady, 'Neighbours and Cousins: Aotearoa-New Zealand's Relationship with the Pacific', in Anne-Marie Brady (ed.), *Small States and the Changing Global Order: New Zealand Faces the Future*, Springer, Cham, 2019; Peter Greener, 'Continuity and Change in New Zealand Defence Policymaking', in Robert Patman, Iati Iati and Balazs Kiglics (eds), *New Zealand and the World: Past, Present and Future*, World Scientific, New Jersey, 2018; and Andrew McRae, '20th Anniversary of NZDF Entering Timor-Leste to Restore Law and Order', Radio New Zealand, 20 September 2019, www.rnz.co.nz/ news/national/399188/20th-anniversary-of-nzdf-entering-timor-leste-to-restore-law-and-order (accessed 12 October 2022).

12 Information on the NZDF's work in the Solomon Islands sourced from Ratuva and Brady, 'Neighbours and Cousins'; Greener, 'Continuity and Change in New Zealand Defence Policymaking'; and David Capie, 'Peacekeeping – Solomon Islands', Te Ara – the Encyclopedia of New Zealand, 2012, www.TeAra.govt.nz/en/ peacekeeping/page-5 (accessed 12 October 2022).

13 Ratuva and Brady, 'Neighbours and Cousins', p.160.

14 Ellen Furnari, Huibert Oldenhuis and Rachel Julian, 'Securing Space for Local Peacebuilding: The Role of International and National Civilian Peacekeepers', *Peacebuilding*, 3, 3 (May 2015), pp.297–313.

15 Rachel Julian and Christine Schweitzer, 'The Origins and Development of Unarmed Civilian Peacekeeping', *Peace Review: A Journal of Social Justice*, 27, 1 (2015), pp.1–8.

16 Molly Wallace, *Security without Weapons: Rethinking Violence, Nonviolent Action, and Civilian Protection*, Routledge, Abingdon, 2016.

17 Ratuva and Brady, 'Neighbours and Cousins'; David Capie, 'Peacekeeping – Bougainville and East Timor', Te Ara – the Encyclopedia of New Zealand, 2012, www.TeAra.govt.nz/en/ peacekeeping/page-4 (accessed 12 October 2022); Antonino Adamo, 'A Cursed and Fragmented Island: History and Conflict Analysis in Bougainville, Papua New Guinea', *Small Wars and Insurgencies*, 29, 1 (2015), pp.164–86.

18 Nicky Hager, *Other People's Wars: New Zealand in Afghanistan, Iraq and the War on Terror*, Craig Potton Publishing, Nelson, 2011.

19 Hager and Stephenson, *Hit and Run*.
20 Ibid.
21 Ibid.

4. The Myth of No Alternatives to Military Force

1 Ministry of Defence, 'Support to Ukraine', August 2022, www.defence.govt.nz/what-we-do/diplomacy-and-deployments/deployment-map/support-to-ukraine/#:~:text=Approximately%20140%20NZDF%20personnel%20will,Ukraine%20in%20its%20self%2Ddefence (accessed 18 October 2022).

2 Erica Chenoweth and Maria J. Stephan, Why Civil Resistance Works: The Strategic Logic of Nonviolent Conflict, Columbia University Press, New York, 2011; Kurt Schock, 'The Practice and Study of Civil Resistance', *Journal of Peace Research*, 50, 3 (2013), pp.277–90, and Gene Sharp, *Waging Nonviolent Struggle: 20th Century Practice and 21st Century Potential*, Extending Horizons Books, Boston, 2005.

3 Chenoweth and Stephan, *Why Civil Resistance Works*.

4 Erica Chenoweth and Kurt Schock, 'Do Contemporaneous Armed Challenges Affect the Outcomes of Mass Nonviolent Campaigns?', *Mobilization: An International Quarterly*, 20, 4 (2015), pp.427–51.

5 Chenoweth and Stephan, Why Civil Resistance Works; Jan Teorell, Determinants of Democratization: Explaining Regime Change in the World, 1972–2006, Cambridge University Press, Cambridge, 2010; Markus Bayer, Felix Bethke and Daniel Lambach, 'The Democratic Dividend of Nonviolent Resistance', Journal of Peace Research, 53, 6 (2016), pp.758–71.

6 Chenoweth and Stephan, *Why Civil Resistance Works*.

7 On nonviolent movements tending to be more democratic, see Schock, 'The Practice and Study of Civil Resistance'.

8 Ned Dobos, *Ethics, Security, and the War-Machine: The True Cost of the Military*, Oxford University Press, Oxford, 2020.

9 Among a large literature, see Charles W. Hoge, Carl A. Castro, Stephen C. Messer, Dennis McGurk, Dave I. Cotting and Robert L. Koffman, 'Combat Duty in Iraq and Afghanistan, Mental Health Problems, and Barriers to Care', *New England Journal of Medicine*, 351, 1 (2004), pp.13–22; H.G. Prigerson, P.K. Maciejewski and R.A. Rosenheck, 'Combat Trauma: Trauma with Highest Risk of Delayed Onset and Unresolved Posttraumatic Stress Disorder Symptoms, Unemployment, and Abuse among Men', *Journal of Nervous and Mental Disease*, 189, 2 (2001), pp.99–108; and H.G. Prigerson, P.K. Maciejewski and R.A.

Rosenheck, 'Population Attributable Fractions of Psychiatric Disorders and Behavioral Outcomes Associated with Combat Exposure among US Men', *American Journal of Public Health*, 92, 1 (2002), p.59.

10   Services Academies: https://alternativeeducation.tki.org.nz/ Services-academies (accessed 3 April 2023).

11   Gene Sharp, *From Dictatorship to Democracy: A Conceptual Framework for Liberation*, first published in Thailand, 1993.

12   Sharp's 198 methods can be found here: www.aeinstein.org/ nonviolentaction/198-methods-of-nonviolent-action (accessed 13 October 2022).

13   See the numerous cases described in the following: Chenoweth and Stephan, *Why Civil Resistance Works*; Schock, 'The Practice and Study of Civil Resistance'; Sharp, *Waging Nonviolent Struggle*.

14   Gene Sharp, *National Security through Civilian-based Defense*, Association for Transarmament Studies, Omaha, NE, 1985, p.9.

15   Thomas Weber, *Gandhi's Peace Army: The Shanti Sena and Unarmed Peacekeeping*, Syracuse University Press, New York, 1996.

16   Maciej Bartkowski, *Nonviolent Civilian Defense to Counter Russian Hybrid Warfare*, Johns Hopkins University Center for Advanced Governmental Studies, 2015.

17   Erica Chenoweth and Stephen Zunes, 'A Nonviolent Alternative for Ukraine', *Foreign Policy*, 28 May 2014, https://foreignpolicy. com/2014/05/28/a-nonviolent-alternative-for-ukraine/ (accessed 13 October 2022).

18   Gene Sharp, *Civilian-based Defense: A Post-military Weapons System*, Princeton University Press, Princeton, NJ, 1990, p.29.

19   George Lakey, 'Ukraine Doesn't Need to Match Russia's Military Might to Defend against Invasion', Waging Nonviolence, 25 February 2022, https://wagingnonviolence.org/2022/02/ ukraine-doesnt-need-to-match-russias-military-might-to-defend-against-invasion/ (accessed 13 October 2022).

20   Lithuanian Ministry of National Defence, *Ką turime žinoti apie pasirengimą ekstremaliosioms situacijoms ir karo metui [What You Need to Know about Preparedness for Emergencies and War]*, Vilnius, 2014, https://kam.lt/en/news_1098/current_issues/ ministry_of_national_defence_issued_third_publication_on_ civil_resistance.html (accessed 17 January 2019).

21   Bartkowski, *Nonviolent Civilian Defense to Counter Russian Hybrid Warfare*; Grazina Miniotaite, 'Lithuania: From Non-violent Liberation towards Non-violent Defence?', *Peace Research: The Canadian Journal of Peace Studies*, 28, 4 (1996), pp.19–36; Robert Burrowes, *The Strategy of Nonviolent Defence:*

A Gandhian Approach, SUNY Press, New York, 1996; Brian Martin, *Social Defence, Social Change*, Freedom Press, London, 1993; Jack Salmon, 'Can Non-violence Be Combined with Military Means for National Defense?', *Journal of Peace Research*, 25, 1 (1988), pp.69–80; Anders Boserup and Andrew Mack, *War Without Weapons: Non-violence in National Defence*, Frances Pinter, London, 1974.

22 Green Party of Aotearoa, 'Defence and Peacekeeping Policy', www.greens.org.nz/defence_and_peacekeeping_policy (accessed 9 May 2023).

23 Furnari, Oldenhui and Julian, 'Securing Space for Local Peacebuilding', pp.297–313.

24 Julian and Schweitzer, 'The Origins and Development of Unarmed Civilian Peacekeeping', p.1.

25 Ibid., p.4.

26 Ibid.

27 Wallace, *Security without Weapons*.

28 Christine Schweitzer (ed.), *Civilian Peacekeeping: A Barely Tapped Resource*, Sozio Publishing, Belm, 2010, pp.7–16.

29 Kara Beckman and Kenneth B. Solberg, *Measuring the Impact of Unarmed Civilian Peacekeeping: A Pilot Study*, report to Nonviolent Peaceforce, November 2013, https://nonviolentpeaceforce.org/wp-content/uploads/2022/06/Final-Report-to-NP-2011-Impact-Assessment-in-Mindanao-18Nov2013-copy.pdf (accessed 17 October 2023).

30 On UCP reducing deaths and deterring violence, see Julian and Schweitzer, 'The Origins and Development of Unarmed Civilian Peacekeeping.'

31 Ellen Furnari, Rachel Julian and Christine Schweitzer, 'Unarmed Civilian Peacekeeping: Effectively Protecting Civilians without Threat of Violence', Working Paper, 2016, www.ssoar.info/ssoar/bitstream/handle/document/48015/ssoar-2016-furnari_et_al-Unarmed_Civilian_Peacekeeping_Effectively_Protecting.pdf?sequence=1 (accessed 18 October 2022).

32 Dwight D. Eisenhower, 'The Chance for Peace', address delivered before the American Society of Newspaper Editors, 16 April 1953, available at Gerhard Peters and John T. Woolley, The American Presidency Project, www.presidency.ucsb.edu/node/231643 (accessed 26 July 2023).

33 Mohammad Alafeshat, 'Navy Frigate Returns to New Zealand after Major Upgrade in Canada', Radio New Zealand, 8 July 2022, www.rnz.co.nz/news/national/470586/navy-frigate-returns-to-new-zealand-after-major-upgrade-in-canada; and 'New Zealand Navy Frigate to Leave Canada Years after Upgrade Began', Radio New Zealand, 17 May 2022, www.rnz.co.nz/news/

national/467270/new-zealand-navy-frigate-to-leave-canada-years-after-upgrade-began (both accessed 12 October 2022).

34   Thomas Manch, 'Navy Will Be Without War Making Frigates the End of 2021', Stuff, 23 February 2021, www.stuff.co.nz/national/politics/124317389/navy-will-be-without-warmaking-frigates-the-end-of-2021 (accessed 26 July 2023).

35   Meriana Johnsen, 'Tauranga Councillor Who Called Treaty of Waitangi a "Joke" Defends Comments', Stuff, 25 October 2019, www.stuff.co.nz/national/116940697/tauranga-councillor-who-called-treaty-of-waitangi-a-joke-defends-comments (accessed 12 October 2022); Rodney Hide, 'Rodney Hide: End the Treaty Gravy Train', *New Zealand Herald*, 12 August 2012, www.nzherald.co.nz/nz/rodney-hide-end-the-treaty-gravy-train/43NRLBKGHZ7YEMUAJGF5NIR4XY/ (accessed 12 October 2022; 'What Are Treaty Settlements and Why Are They Needed?', Te Tai: Treaty Settlement Stories, https://teara.govt.nz/en/te-tai/about-treaty-settlements (accessed 12 October 2022).

36   Sam Olley, 'Sewage Leaking into Whangārei Hospital Medical Wing's Walls', Radio New Zealand, 13 November 2021, www.rnz.co.nz/news/national/455622/sewage-leaking-into-whangarei-hospital-medical-wing-s-walls (accessed 12 October 2022); Eileen Goodwin, 'Hospital Leaks Worse than Stated', *Otago Daily Times*, 16 February 2017, www.odt.co.nz/news/dunedin/health/hospital-leaks-worse-stated (accessed 12 October 2022); '"Unprecedented Stress, Chaotic" – Emergency Depts Overcrowded', Radio New Zealand, 20 June 2022, www.rnz.co.nz/national/programmes/checkpoint/audio/2018846554/unprecedented-stress-chaotic-emergency-depts-overcrowded (accessed 12 October 2022).

37   Tina Morrison, 'Private Healthcare Benefits when Public Falls Short', Stuff, 13 July 2022, www.stuff.co.nz/business/129241178/private-healthcare-benefits-when-public-falls-short (accessed 12 October 2022).

38   Anonymous, 'Building a New Hospital is Cheap at any Price', The Spinoff, 29 June 2022, https://thespinoff.co.nz/business/29-06-2022/building-a-new-hospital-is-cheap-at-any-price (accessed 26 July 2023).

39   Sam Olley, 'Government Sets Aside $572m for Whangārei Hospital', Radio New Zealand, 4 March 2022, www.rnz.co.nz/news/national/462715/government-sets-aside-572m-for-whangarei-hospital (accessed 12 October 22).

40   Hon. Andrew Little, 'Dunedin Hospital Construction Signals Start of Major Health Infrastructure Work', press release, 3 June 2022, www.beehive.govt.nz/release/dunedin-hospital-

construction-signals-start-major-health-infrastructure-work
(accessed 17 July 2023).

41   Stockholm International Peace Research Institute, 'World
Military Expenditure Reaches New Record High as European
Spending Surges', press release, 24 April 2023, www.sipri.
org/media/press-release/2023/world-military-expenditure-
reaches-new-record-high-european-spending-surges (accessed
17 July 2023); Belinda Goldsmith, 'Just 10 Percent of World
Military Spending Could Knock Off Poverty: Think Tank',
Reuters, 5 April 2016, www.reuters.com/article/us-global-
military-goals/just-10-percent-of-world-military-spending-
could-knock-off-poverty-think-tank-idUSKCN0X12EQ (accessed
18 October 2022).

42   Security and Intelligence Group, *National Plan to Address
Cybercrime*, Security and Intelligence Group, Wellington, 2015,
pp.6–7, www.dpmc.govt.nz/sites/default/files/2017-03/nz-cyber-
security-cybercrime-plan-december-2015.pdf (accessed 18
October 2022).

43   Ministry of Defence, *Defence Assessment 2014*, Wellington,
2015, p.25, www.defence.govt.nz/assets/Uploads/802ce528c8/
defence- assessment- 2014-public.pdf (accessed 7 October
2022); Department of the Prime Minister and Cabinet, *Briefing
to Incoming Minister Responsible for Cyber Security Policy*,
Department of the Prime Minister and Cabinet, Wellington,
2017, p.14, www.dpmc.govt.nz/sites/default/files/2017-12/
bim-cyber-security-policy-oct-2017.pdf (accessed 18 October
2022).

44   A. Martinez Casares and J. Guyler Delva, 'Haitian Army Set to
Make Controversial Return after Two Decades', Reuters, 19
November 2017, www.reuters.com/article/us-haiti-military/
haitian-army-set-to-make-controversial-return-after-two-
decades-idUSKBN1DJ01M (accesed 18 October 2022); J.
Guyler Delva, 'Haiti Installs New High Command for Planned
5,000-strong Army', Reuters, 28 March 2018, www.reuters.com/
article/us-haiti-military/haiti-installs-new-high-command-
for-planned-5000-strong-army-idUSKBN1H40CV (accessed 18
October 2022).

45   Foreign Affairs, Defence and Trade Committee, *Inquiry into
New Zealand's Relationship with South Pacific Countries*, Foreign
Affairs, Defence and Trade Committee, Wellington, 2010,
www.parliament.nz/resource/en-nz/49DBSCH_SCR4945_1/
a1e8715f6c270cf5ff075f2d42f4e19f92aef10d (accessed 18 October
2022).

46   Jason Hickel, 'Want to Avert the Apocalypse? Take Lessons from
Costa Rica', *The Guardian*, 7 October 2017, www.theguardian.

com/working-in-development/2017/oct/07/how-to-avert-the-apocalypse-take-lessons-from-costa-rica (accessed 18 October 2022).
47   Ibid., emphasis added.

Conclusion: Replacing Myth with Reality

1   Richard Jackson, 'The Need to Diversify New Zealand's War Narratives', Briefing Papers, AUT, 14 November 2018, https://briefingpapers.co.nz/the-need-to-diversify-new-zealands-war-narratives (accessed 18 October 2022).

Acknowledgements

The arguments presented in this book were first made by Griffin Leonard and Joseph Llewellyn at a conference in 2017 held at the University of Otago's National Centre for Peace and Conflict Studies. Later that year, we presented a revised version of the paper, entitled 'Imagining Nonviolent Foreign Policy in a Violent World', at the Small States and the Changing Global Order: New Zealand Faces the Future conference/hui, at the University of Canterbury. The research was then published as a book chapter, 'Meeting New Zealand's Peace and Security Challenges through Disarmament and Nonviolence', in Anne-Marie Brady (ed.), *Small States and the Changing Global Order: New Zealand Faces the Future* (Springer, New York, 2019, pp.345–61). We are grateful to all those who commented and made helpful suggestions about the arguments and research along the way. We are also grateful to the University of Otago for support while we wrote this book.

About the Authors

Griffin Manawaroa Leonard (Te Arawa) obtained his PhD from the National Centre for Peace and Conflict Studies at the University of Otago. Following his PhD, he worked as an independent researcher and has published peer-reviewed material on a variety of subjects including international relations, public health and adult learning. He has participated in a number of activist and community development groups dedicated to social justice and nonviolence.

Joseph Llewellyn completed his PhD at the National Centre for Peace and Conflict Studies at the University of Otago. His work focuses on nonviolence, pacifism, anarchism, colonial violence, equity and military abolition. Before conducting his PhD research, Joseph completed a Master of Arts and a Post-Graduate Diploma in Peace and Conflict Studies at the National Centre for Peace and Conflict Studies. Before that, he trained as an occupational therapist. He has been a part of multiple peace-related activist groups, projects and campaigns.

Richard Jackson holds the Leading Thinkers Chair in Peace Studies at the University of Otago. He lectures on critical terrorism studies and critical peace studies at the National Centre for Peace and Conflict Studies. He is the author or editor of fifteen books and more than a hundred articles and book chapters on pacifism and nonviolence, conflict resolution, war and terrorism. He is the editor of the journal *Critical Studies on Terrorism* and commentates regularly in the media on international security issues. He is also the author of a novel based on his research, *Confessions of a Terrorist* (Zed Books, 2014).

About BWB Texts

BWB Texts are short books on big subjects for Aotearoa New Zealand. Over 100 Texts have been published since the series launched in 2013, available in print and digital formats. These can be purchased from all good bookstores and online from www.bwb.co.nz. To celebrate the milestone of publishing 100 Texts, starting from the 101st Text, each new title will feature its sequential number on the front cover.

BWB Texts include:

Encounters Across Time
Judith Binney

Introducing The Women's Suffrage Petition
Edited by Jared Davidson, historical essay by Barbara Brookes

Introducing Te Tiriti o Waitangi
Edited by Jared Davidson, historical essay by Claudia Orange

Introducing He Whakaputanga: He Tohu Series
Edited by Jared Davidson, historical essay by Vincent O'Malley

Privilege in Perpetuity: Exploding a Pākehā Myth
Peter Meihana

The Best of E-Tangata, Volume Two
Tapu Misa and Gary Wilson (eds)

More Zeros and Ones: Digital Technology, Maintenance and Equity in Aotearoa New Zealand
Anna Pendergrast and Kelly Pendergrast (eds)

Pesticides and Health: How New Zealand Fails in Environmental Protection
Neil Pearce

Fragments from a Contested Past: Remembrance, Denial and New Zealand History
Joanna Kidman, Vincent O'Malley, Liana MacDonald, Tom Roa and Keziah Wallis

Kārearea
Māmari Stephens

Kāinga: People, Land, Belonging
Paul Tapsell

He Pou Hiringa: Grounding Science and Technology in Te Ao Māori
Maria Amoamo, Merata Kawharu and Katharina Ruckstuhl (eds)

The History of a Riot
Jared Davidson

100% Pure Future: New Zealand Tourism Renewed
Sarah Bennett (ed.)

Two Hundred and Fifty Ways to Start an Essay about Captain Cook
Alice Te Punga Somerville

Living with the Climate Crisis: Voices from Aotearoa
Tom Doig (ed.)

The Platform: The Radical Legacy of the Polynesian Panthers
Melani Anae

Shouting Zeros and Ones: Digital Technology, Ethics and Policy in New Zealand
Andrew Chen (ed.)

Beyond These Shores: Aotearoa and the World
Nina Hall (ed.)

Imagining Decolonisation
Various

The Climate Dispossessed: Justice for the Pacific in Aotearoa?
Teall Crossen

First published in 2023 by Bridget Williams Books Ltd
PO Box 12474, Wellington 6144, New Zealand
www.bwb.co.nz, info@bwb.co.nz.

ISBN 9781991033529 (Paperback), ISBN 9781991033536 (EPUB),
ISBN 9781991033543 (Kindle), ISBN 9781991033550 (PDF)
DOI https://doi.org/10.7810/9781991033529

A catalogue record for this book is available from the National
Library of New Zealand. Kei te pātengi raraunga o Te Puna Mātauranga
o Aotearoa te whakarārangi o tēnei pukapuka.

The publisher warmly acknowledges the significance of the ongoing
support provided by the Bridget Williams Books Publishing Trust.
The generous contribution from Ockham Residential for the BWB Texts
series is gratefully acknowledged.

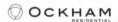

Publisher: Tom Rennie
Editor: Anna Hodge
Cover design: Neil Pardington Design
Internal design and typesetting: Katrina Duncan
Printer: Blue Star, Wellington